MW01120747

10 Minute Guide to
Excel 4

Mike Miller
Revised by Jennifer Flynn

SAMS

A Division of Prentice Hall Computer Publishing

11711 North College, Carmel, Indiana 46032 USA

©1992 by SAMS

International Standard Book Number: 0-672-30126-1
Library of Congress Catalog Card Number: 92-80460

95 94 93 92   8 7 6 5 4 3 2 1

Interpretation of the printing code: the rightmost double-digit number is the year of the book's first printing; the rightmost single-digit number is the number of the book's printing. For example, a printing code of 92-1 shows that this copy of the book was printed during the first printing of the book in 1992.

Publisher: *Richard K. Swadley*
Associate Publisher: *Marie Butler-Knight*
Managing Editor: *Elizabeth Keaffaber*
Acquisitions Editor: *Steven R. Poland*
Senior Development Editor: *Lisa Bucki*
Manuscript Editor: *Howard Peirce*
Editorial Assistant: *Hilary Adams*
Cover Design: *Dan Armstrong*
Designer: *Michele Laseau*
Indexer: *Tina Trettin*
Production Team: *Mike Britton, Paula Carroll, Brad Chinn, Joelynn Gifford, Denny Hager, Debbie Hanna, Audra Hershman, Carrie Keesling, David McKenna, Matthew Morrill, Anne Owen, Juli Pavey, Caroline Roop, Johnna VanHoose, Corinne Walls, Jenny Watson*

Special thanks to Hilary Adams for assuring the technical accuracy of this book.

Screen reproductions in this book were created by means of the program Collage Plus from Inner Media, Inc., Hollis, NH.

Printed in the United States of America

Contents

Introduction

Perhaps you walked into work this morning to find that a new program has been installed on your computer. Your boss wants you to use this new program, Microsoft Excel 4.0, to create the monthly sales report. What do you do?

A few things are certain:

- You need a method of finding your way around Excel quickly and easily.

- You need to identify and learn the tasks necessary to accomplish your particular goals.

- You need a clear-cut, plain-English guide to the basic features of the program.

You need the *10 Minute Guide to Excel 4 for Windows*.

What Is the 10 Minute Guide?

The *10 Minute Guide* series is designed to help you learn new programs quickly and easily. Through a series of lessons which take less than 10 minutes each, you can quickly master the basic skills needed to produce complete worksheets using Microsoft Excel.

Best of all, you do not have to spend time figuring out what to learn. All the most important tasks are covered in this *10 Minute Guide*. There's no need for long classes or thick manuals. Learn the skills you need in short, easy-to-follow lessons.

Conventions Used in This Book

Each of the lessons in this Guide includes step-by-step instructions for performing a specific task. The following icons are included to help you quickly identify particular types of information:

Plain English These definitions appear wherever a new term is introduced. You'll quickly learn the terms you need to understand Microsoft Excel.

Panic Button These identify areas where new users might run into trouble, and offer practical solutions to potential problems.

Timesaver Tips These tips offer you shortcuts and hints for using the program efficiently and effectively.

In addition, Version 4.0 icons help you identify features that are new to Microsoft Excel 4.0. You can quickly take advantage of the latest timesaving features of Excel.

The following conventions are also used:

On-screen text	On-screen text will appear in a special monospace font.
What you type	Information you type will appear in a bold, color, monospace font.
Items you select	Items you select or keys you press will appear in color.
Selection keys	Boldface letters within a menu, command, or option name indicate selection keys for keyboard shortcuts. These correspond to the underlined letters on-screen.

Using This Book

On the inside front cover of this book, you will find instructions for installing Microsoft Excel on your system. The inside back cover features a guide to the Toolbars used with Microsoft Excel.

This book contains over 20 lessons, which each cover a specific task for using Microsoft Excel. You should complete each of the lessons in order until you feel comfortable using the program. After lesson 9, you may wish to skip around and complete only those lessons you need for your work.

For Further Reference . . .

If you wish a more detailed guide to using Microsoft Excel, I suggest the following books from Sams:

> *The First Book of Microsoft Excel 4* by Chris Van Buren, revised by Trudi Reisner.
>
> The *10 Minute Guide to Windows 3.1*, by Kate Barnes.

Acknowledgments

To all the wonderful people at Sams, especially Lisa Bucki, for her clear insight and guidance, Steve Poland for prodding me to do this, and Marie Bulter-Knight, for giving me my chance.

Trademarks

All terms mentioned in this book that are known to be trademarks or service marks are listed below. In addition, terms suspected of being trademarks or service marks have been appropriately capitalized. Sams cannot attest to the accuracy of this information. Use of a term in this book should not be regarded as affecting the validity of any trademark or service mark.

MS-DOS, Windows, Excel, and Toolbar are trademarks of Microsoft Corporation.

Lessons

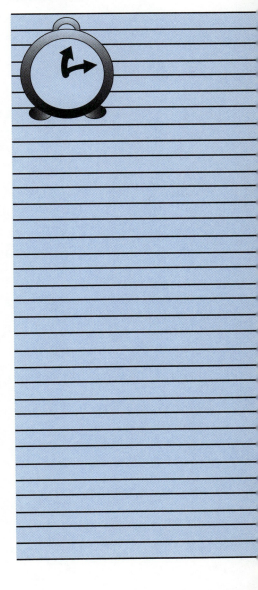

Lesson 1

Starting and Exiting Excel

In this lesson you will learn how to start and exit Excel. You also will learn the parts of an Excel worksheet window, and how to use the mouse.

Starting Excel

Starting Excel is like starting any other Windows program. To start Excel, Windows must be running. To start Windows:

1. Type **WIN** at the DOS prompt.

2. Press Enter.

   Launch the Excel program from the Program Manager. The Program Manager is the main program within Windows. You use the Program Manager to run your other application programs and organize them into small groups. When you start Windows, the Program Manager is usually open and running. If the Program Manager window is not open:

   • Double-click on the Program Manager icon, or press Tab until the Program Manager icon is selected and press Enter.

1

Double-click   Double-clicking on a program icon will start the program. An icon is a small picture which represents something such as a program, a file, or a program group. To double-click, press the left mouse button two times in rapid succession.

With the Program Manager window open, start the Excel program:

1. To open the program group window which holds the Excel icon:

   • Press Tab to select the group icon and press Enter.

   Or

   • Double-click on the group icon (see Figure 1.1).

2. To select the Microsoft Excel icon:

   • Press Tab to highlight the icon and press Enter.

   Or

   • Double-click on the icon with the mouse.

The Excel opening screen appears with a blank worksheet titled Sheet1 (see Figure 1.2). The Excel program is now ready for you to use.

Worksheet   A worksheet is a file which is divided into cells; each individual cell is the intersection of a horizontal row and a vertical column.

The Excel program group window

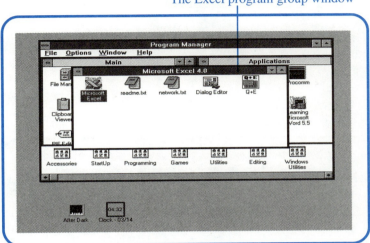

Figure 1.1   The Program Manager with the Excel group window open.

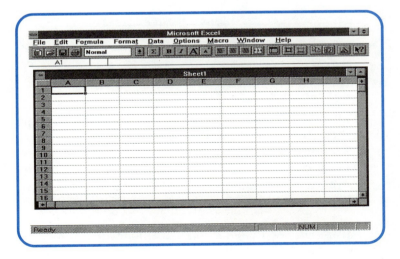

Figure 1.2   Excel's opening screen.

The Excel Worksheet Screen

The typical Excel worksheet screen, shown in Figure 1.3, has many parts.

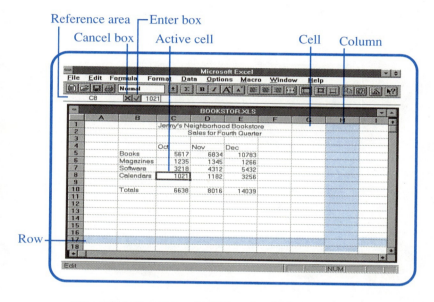

Figure 1.3 A typical Excel window.

Cell   A single box where data is entered. A cell is the intersection of a column and a row.

Active cell   The active cell will be affected by the current action—such as keystrokes or menu commands. The active cell is highlighted by a dark border.

Rows   Rows are horizontal sections which run down the length of a worksheet, numbered consecutively from 1 through 16384.

Columns   Columns are vertical sections which run across a worksheet, numbered consecutively from A through Z, then AA, AB, and on through IV.

Reference area   Displays the name of the active cell. Cells are referenced first by column, and then by row— for example, cell A4 is the cell located in column A, row 4.

Formula bar   Displays either the data or the formula for the contents of the active cell. You will be learning more about formulas in Lesson 10.

Cancel box   Click here to cancel an entry to the active cell.

Enter box   Click here to accept an entry to the active cell.

Toolbar   Contains many icons (tools) you click on to perform various tasks (such as formatting and justification). The individual tools will be described in Lesson 4.

Basic Mouse Techniques

When using any Windows program, you should use a mouse to perform most of the basic tasks. A mouse is a device attached to your computer which controls a pointer on your screen. To move the pointer to the left, move the mouse to the left. To move the pointer to the right, move the mouse to the right, and so on. To initiate most actions with the mouse, you either click or double-click.

Click   To click with the mouse, position the mouse pointer and press the left button once. To select a cell, click on the cell.

Double-click   To double-click with the mouse, press the left button twice in rapid succession.

Some actions require that you drag the mouse. For example, you can drag the mouse to select several cells.

Drag   To drag with the mouse, move the mouse pointer to the starting position. Now click and hold the left mouse button. Drag the mouse pointer to the ending position and release the left button.

Exiting Excel

To exit Excel and return to Windows, follow these steps:

1. Pull down the File menu by pressing Alt-F or clicking on File.

2. Select the Exit command by clicking on it or pressing X. If you have unsaved files open, Excel will prompt you to save them. You will learn more about saving worksheet files in Lesson 5. Select the appropriate command button. Excel will then close and return you to Windows.

In this lesson, you learned how to start and exit Excel. You also learned about the main parts of the Excel window, and how to use a mouse. In the next lesson you will learn how to control worksheet windows.

Lesson 2

Controlling Worksheet Windows

In this lesson you will learn the parts of a window, and how to resize and move them.

Parts of a Window

One of the wonderful things about Windows programs is that they share a common user interface. This means that when you learn the basic parts of an Excel 4 for Windows window, you will be able to recognize those parts in every Windows program. The parts of the Excel program window are illustrated Figure 2.1.

Program window This window frames the tools and menus for the entire application.

Worksheet window This window frames the controls and information for the worksheet file being worked on. You may have multiple worksheet windows open at one time.

Title bar This displays the title for the window, which will either be the name of the program (program window), or the name of the current worksheet (worksheet window).

Menu bar   Displays the names of the different menus for the current application. These menus contain commands which can be used to manipulate worksheets.

Control button   Clicking here will display a menu with commands for resizing, closing, and moving windows.

Minimize button   Click here to reduce the window to an icon at the bottom of your screen.

Maximize button   Click here to increase the window to fill your screen.

Restore button   Click here to restore the window to its previous size.

Scroll bars   Located along the bottom and right sides of the worksheet window, you can click on the arrows to display adjacent areas of the worksheet.

Status bar   The right side displays the status of the Caps Lock, Num Lock, and Scroll Lock keys. The left side displays information about the current command.

The Control Menu

The Control menu for the program contains commands used for resizing, closing, and moving the program window. Table 2.1 describes these commands. To open the Control menu, click on it with the mouse. To open it with the keyboard, press the Alt key, followed by the space bar.

Program control button

Worksheet window control menu

Menu bar   Title bar   Program minimize button

Program maximize/restore button

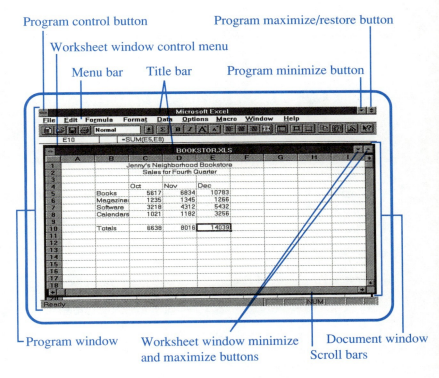

Program window   Worksheet window minimize   Document window
                   and maximize buttons   Scroll bars

Figure 2.1 Parts of the Program window.

Table 2.1 The program window Control menu commands.

Command	Keyboard Command	Description
Restore	F5	Restores the window to its previous size.
Move	F7	Use the arrow keys to move the window to the desired position.

continues

Table 2.1 Continued

Command	Keyboard Command	Description
Size	F8	Use the arrow keys to change the size of the window.
Minimize	F9	Reduces the window to an icon at the bottom of the screen. Double-click on this icon to restore the window.
Maximize	F10	Causes the window to fill the entire screen.
Close	Alt-F4	Closes the window. You will be prompted to save data before the window is closed.
Switch To	Ctrl-Esc	Displays the Windows Task List. Use this command to switch to another program. Excel will be temporarily "frozen" until you return to it.
Run		Use this command to start any program.

Most of these commands can also be performed with the mouse. For example, you can click on the Restore button of a window to restore it to its previous size. These commands can also be performed by pressing the indicated keyboard keys. For example, to restore a window using the keyboard, press and hold the Ctrl key, press the F5 key, and release both keys.

Excel's worksheet window Control menu has all the commands listed in Table 2.1 (except the Switch To and Run commands) as well as two additional commands, described in Table 2.2. To open the worksheet Control menu, click on it with the mouse. To open it with the keyboard, press the Alt key, followed by the minus sign.

Table 2.2 Excel's worksheet Control menu
commands.

Command	Keyboard Command	Description
Restore	Ctrl-F5	Restores the window to its previous size.
Move	Ctrl-F7	Use the arrow keys to move the window to the desired position.
Size	Ctrl-F8	Use the arrow keys to change the size of the window.
Mi**n**imize	Ctrl-F9	Reduces the window to an icon at the bottom of the screen. Double-click on this icon to restore the window.
Maximize	Ctrl-F10	Causes the window to fill the entire screen.
Close	Alt-F4	Closes the window. You will be prompted to save data before the window is closed.
Next Window	Ctrl-F6	Use this command to switch between worksheets. You'll learn more about this in Lesson 5.
Split		Divides the screen in two so that you can work either on two worksheets or two parts of the same worksheet at once.

While you're using Excel, you'll often need to change
the size and location of worksheet windows. The following
sections explain how.

Resizing a Worksheet Window

You may adjust the size of any window by using the mouse or the keyboard. To resize a window using the mouse:

1. Move the mouse pointer to the appropriate border of the window to be resized. The mouse pointer will change from an arrow to a double-headed arrow.

2. Press and hold the left mouse button.

3. Drag the border to its new location.

4. Release the left button.

5. The window will resize itself to fit the new borders.

Two at Once To move both the horizontal and vertical borders at the same time, start with the mouse pointer at one corner. When you drag the mouse, the corner will move, dragging both borders with it.

To resize a worksheet window with the keyboard:

1. Open the Control menu for the window.

2. Choose Size by clicking on it or pressing **S**. The pointer will change into a four-headed arrow.

3. Press any of the arrow keys to select the appropriate border.

4. Continue to press the arrow key until the window is the size you want and press Enter.

Maximizing, Minimizing, and Restoring

You can also maximize, minimize, and restore the size of any worksheet window with either the mouse or the keyboard.

Clear the Area! When working with multiple worksheets, you can temporarily "put the worksheet aside" by minimizing it. When you need to use the worksheet again, restore it.

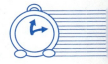

To minimize, maximize, or restore with the mouse:

1. Click on the Minimize, Maximize, or Restore button (see Figure 2.1).

2. To restore a minimized window, double-click on the window's icon.

To minimize, maximize, or restore with the keyboard:

1. Open the Control menu for the window.

2. Select the appropriate command from the Control menu by pressing the underlined letter in the command name.

You can also use one of the following keyboard short-cuts:

Command	Shortcut key
Minimize	Ctrl-F9
Maximize	Ctrl-F10
Restore	Ctrl-F5

Moving a Worksheet Window

You can move a worksheet window by using either the mouse or the keyboard.

To move a window with the mouse:

1. Click on the window's title bar.

2. While holding the left button down, drag the window to its new location.

3. Release the left mouse button.

To move a window with the keyboard:

1. Display the window's Control menu. Select Move by pressing M or press Ctrl-F7. The pointer will change to a four-headed arrow.

2. Use the arrow keys to move the window to its new location.

3. When the window has been relocated, press Enter.

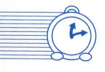

Arranging Multiple Windows   Use the Arrange command on the Window menu to arrange multiple windows. You can choose to arrange the windows Vertically (from left to right), Horizontally (from top to bottom), or Tiled (in small rectangles to fit the screen).

In this lesson, you learned the parts of a typical window, and how to move and resize them to your own specifications. In the next lesson, you will learn how to use menus and dialog boxes.

Lesson 3
Using Menus and Dialog Boxes

In this lesson, you will learn about the Excel menus and how to use them. Save time with Excel 4.0's new shortcut menus. You will also learn how to make selections in dialog boxes.

Excel's Menu Structure

All of Excel's many commands can be invoked from its menu system. The commands are found on pull-down menus that appear under the menu bar when selected. Excel's main menu bar contains nine menus:

File   Contains file-related commands, such as those used for saving, opening, and closing files. Also contains commands for printing worksheets.

Edit   Contains editing commands, such as Copy, Cut, Paste, and Fill.

Formula   Contains commands that allow you to create formulas and what-if situations for your worksheet.

Format   Contains commands that allow you to customize the data in your worksheet or chart, and to customize its appearance.

Data   Contains commands that allow you to sort, find, and extract records from your data.

Options   Contains commands that customize your worksheet and work environment.

Macro   Contains commands for creating short programs that repeat often-used tasks.

Window   Contains commands that allow you to arrange the various worksheet windows or to zoom into a specific area.

Help   Accesses the on-line help system.

Selecting Menu Commands

Commands can be selected from the menus using the keyboard or the mouse. Throughout the rest of this book, when you are asked to "select" a command from a menu, it means to use any of the methods described next to choose a command.

Selecting a command has three results:

- The command will be executed.

- The command will be toggled. A toggle is like a light switch; it can only be on or off. A command of this type will be displayed with a check mark in front of it if it is on.

- The command will display a small box called a dialog box, where you will have to make several additional selections. A command of this type will be displayed with an ellipsis (. . .) to the right of it. You will learn about dialog boxes later in this lesson.

To select commands using the mouse:

1. Open the menu by clicking once on the menu name in the menu bar (see Figure 3.1).

2. Click on the correct command.

Select the menu name. The pull-down menu appears.

Select a command

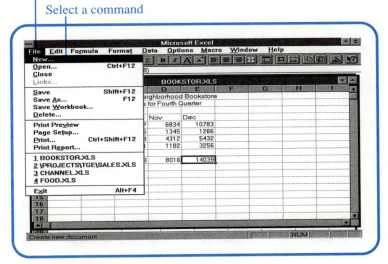

Figure 3.1 Excel's File menu.

One-Step Selection You can select a menu option in one step by pressing the left button as you move down the menu. Release the button when the pointer is on the correct menu option.

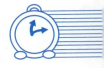

17

To select options using the keyboard:

1. Press the Alt key.

2. Press the highlighted letter from the menu you wish to select. For example, Press Alt-F to activate the **F**ile menu.

3. Use ↑ and ↓ to move to the desired option and then press Enter, or press the highlighted letter for that option. For example, to select the **O**pen option from the **F**ile menu, move down to the **O**pen option and press Enter, or press O.

Using Shifted Commands

There are a few additional commands that can only be selected with the use of the Shift key. These commands are listed in Table 3.1.

Table 3.1   Excel's Shifted Commands

Regular Comamnd	Shifted Command	Purpose of Shifted Command
File Close	File Close All	Close all open worksheets.
Edit Copy	Edit Copy Picture	Place copy of picture in memory so that it can be copied to another location.
Edit Fill Right	Edit Fill Left	Copy (fill) data to cells to the left.
Edit Fill Down	Edit Fill Up	Copy (fill) data to cells above.
Edit Paste	Edit Paste Picture	Place copy of picture from memory to current location in worksheet.

18

Regular Comamnd	Shifted Command	Purpose of Shifted Command
Edit Paste Link	Edit Paste Picture Link	Place copy of picture to current location, with a link to the program that created it.

To choose Shifted commands:

1. Hold down the Shift key.

2. Activate the menu you want.

3. Select the command you want.

Using Dialog Boxes

Certain menu commands require additional information before they can be executed by the program. These menu options are usually followed by an ellipsis (. . .), as in the File Save As . . . option. When you choose one of these commands, Excel displays a dialog box like the one shown in Figure 3.2.

In a dialog box, you will be presented with many ways to select options. You may change options by using the mouse or the keyboard. When using the keyboard, use the Tab key to move the highlight from option to option or press Alt and the highlighted letter of the choice you wish to change, as in Color (Alt-C). Some of the most common ways that options are presented include:

List boxes   Used when many choices are possible, such as the font names. Select your choice from the list by clicking on it with the mouse, or use ↑ and ↓.

19

Option buttons   Used to group mutually exclusive options, such as left or right alignment. Click once with the mouse (or highlight and press Enter) to turn an option on (the round button will fill), or use the arrow keys to move the dot (the filled button) from choice to choice.

Check boxes   Used to group similar options, such as Bold and Italic. Click once with the mouse (or highlight and press the space bar) to turn an option on (an x will appear) or off.

Text boxes   Used for typing a unique selection, such as a file name.

Drop-down list box   This is like other list boxes, but the list will not display until activated. To activate the list, click on it with the mouse. With the keyboard, move to the list with the Tab key and press Alt-↓ to reveal the list. Highlight the option you want from the list by using ↑ and ↓.

Command buttons   Generally used to indicate OK ("accept changes") or Cancel ("return to worksheet; do not accept changes"), command buttons can also indicate another dialog box (for example, **O**ptions . . .).

Using Shortcut Menus

Excel 4.0 introduces a new concept in menu selection: Shortcut menus. These menus appear near the selected cell or object, and contain the commands available for editing and formatting the selection. A Shortcut menu appears in Figure 3.3.

Check boxes   List box   Text box   Drop-down list box   Command buttons

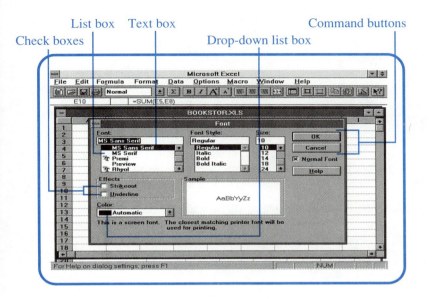

Figure 3.2   A typical dialog box.

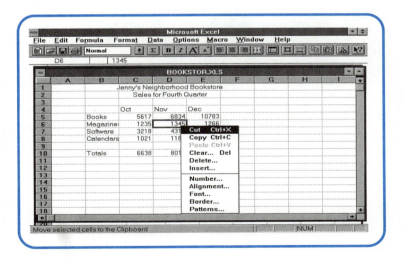

Figure 3.3   A Shortcut menu.

To open a Shortcut menu with the mouse:

1. With a cell, range, or object selected, point to it and click the right mouse button.

2. When the menu appears, click on the command you want.

To open a Shortcut menu with the keyboard:

1. With a cell, range, or object selected, press Shift-F10.

2. When the menu appears, use ↑ and ↓ to select the option you wish.

You will use the Shortcut menus in later lessons. In this lesson, you learned about menus and dialog boxes, and how to select options from them. In the next lesson, you will learn how to use the Toolbar.

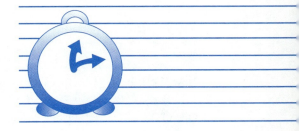

Using the Toolbar

In this lesson, you will learn how to use Excel's Toolbars to save time when you work. You will also learn how to arrange them to suit your taste.

Selecting Standard Toolbar Tools

Excel displays the Standard Toolbar (see Figure 4.1) by default. To select a tool from a Toolbar, click on that tool with the mouse.

What Is a Toolbar? An Excel Toolbar is a collection of tools or shortcut icons displayed in a long bar which can be moved and reshaped to suit your needs.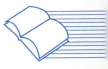

Copy ——┐   ┌—— Paste

Figure 4.1 The Excel Standard Toolbar.

The Standard Toolbar allows you to execute the most often used menu commands, as shown in Table 4.1:

23

Table 4.1 The Tools in the Standard Toolbar

Tool	Description
New Worksheet	Opens a new worksheet file (see Lesson 5)
Open File	Opens an existing document (see Lesson 5)
Save File	Saves an existing document (see Lesson 5)
Print File	Prints your current document (see Lesson 12)
Style Box	Applies a style to the current cell (see Lesson 17)
Autosum	Sums (totals) the cells above and to the left of the current cell (see Lesson 12)
Bold	Makes the selected text bold (see Lesson 14)
Italic	Makes the selected text italic (see Lesson 14)
Increase Font Size	Increases the size of selected text to the next available size (see Lesson 14)
Decrease Font Size	Decreases the size of selected text to the next available size (see Lesson 14)
Left Align	Aligns the selected text on the left (see Lesson 15)
Center Align	Centers the selected text (see Lesson 15)
Right Align	Aligns the selected text on the right (see Lesson 15)
Center Across Columns	Centers the selected text over the indicated columns (see Lesson 15)
Auto Format	Automatically formats the various elements of a table (see Lesson 15)
Outline Border	Places an outline around the selected cells (see Lesson 15)

Tool	Description
Bottom Border	Places a line under the selected cells (see Lesson 15)
Copy Tool	Copies the selected cells or objects to the clipboard (same as Copy command)
Paste Formats	Pastes the formats of cells copied to the clipboard
ChartWizard	Starts the ChartWizard (see Lesson 18)
Help	Use this tool to get help on any Excel menu, or any part of an Excel worksheet.

Hiding and Displaying the Standard Toolbar

To hide a Toolbar, you can use the Options menu or the Shortcut menu.

To use the Options menu to hide or display a Toolbar:

1. Click on the Options menu or press Alt-O.

2. Click on Toolbars, or press O. The Show Toolbars dialog box appears.

3. Select the Toolbar you would like to hide or display.

4. To hide a Toolbar, choose Hide or press Alt-I. To display a Toolbar, choose Show or press Alt-S.

To use the Shortcut menu to hide or display a Toolbar:

1. Move the mouse pointer to an open space within the Toolbar.

2. Display the Shortcut menu by clicking with the right mouse button (see Figure 4.2).

3. Excel places a check mark next to the name of a displayed Toolbar. To remove a check mark (to hide a Toolbar), or to add a check mark (to display a Toolbar), select the name of the Toolbar from the Shortcut menu.

Figure 4.2   The Standard Toolbar Shortcut menu.

Using Other Toolbars

Excel has a total of nine Toolbars, including the Standard Toolbar shown in Figure 4.1. The additional Toolbars are listed below:

Formatting   Shortcuts that include font selection, number formats, and shading.

Utility   Common commands such as Copy, Repeat, and Undo.

Chart   Commands used in customizing charts.

Drawing   Tools used to draw simple figures.

Microsoft Excel 3.0   The standard Toolbar used in Excel Version 3.0.

Macro   Used in creating macros, which are named series of commands that you program.

Macro Paused   Used when a running macro is paused.

You may display any or all of the Toolbars in your work area. You can also move and resize the Toolbars to suit your taste.

Is It Getting Crowded in Here?   Try to get in the habit of displaying only the Toolbars you need. Displaying a lot of unnecessary Toolbars will reduce your screen space and use memory.

Moving Toolbars

After you have displayed the Toolbars which you would like to use, you may position them in your work area where they are most convenient. Figure 4.3 shows a worksheet with three Toolbars in various areas.

When a Toolbar is initially displayed, it is placed at the top or bottom of the work area. To move a Toolbar:

1. Move the mouse pointer to an open space on the Toolbar.

2. Press and hold the left mouse button to drag the Toolbar to the new location. If you drag it close to an edge, the Toolbar will snap into the *Toolbar dock*.

Floating Toolbars   Drawing Toolbar in toolbar dock

Standard Toolbar

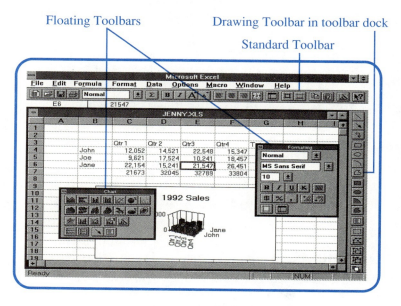

Figure 4.3 An Excel worksheet displaying three Toolbars.

Toolbar Dock The Toolbar dock is located along each edge of the work area. When a Toolbar is moved close to the Toolbar dock, it will automatically snap into place along that edge. The Drawing Toolbar shown in Figure 4.3 is in the right Toolbar dock.

Floating Toolbars Any Toolbars that are not in a Toolbar dock are floating Toolbars. The Utility and Chart Toolbars shown in Figure 4.3 are floating Toolbars.

Resizing Toolbars

To resize a Toolbar, grab it by the edge like any window, and drag that edge to the new size. After a Toolbar has been resized, the tools within it will be rearranged to accommodate the new size. The Utility Toolbar shown in Figure 4.3 has been resized.

Using the Shift Command with Toolbar Tools

Some tools have "twins" that represent the opposite action. You can toggle between twin tools by using the Shift key. To switch between the actions of twin tools, hold down the Shift key as you click on the tool. For example, to draw a filled circle with the Circle tool, hold down the Shift key when you click on it. Likewise, to draw a circle with the Filled Circle Tool, hold down the Shift key as you click on it.

Put Away those Tools! If you like using the Shift key with tools, save room on your Toolbars by removing one of each of the twin tools.

Tool	Twin Tool	Toolbar
Arc	Filled Arc	Drawing
Bring to Front	Send to Back	Drawing
Decrease Decimal	Increase Decimal	Formatting
Decrease Font Size	Increase Font Size	Standard
Delete	Insert	(can add to any Toolbar)
Delete Column	Insert Column	(can add to any Toolbar)
Delete Row	Insert Row	(can add to any Toolbar)

Tool	Twin Tool	Toolbar
Filled Freehand Polygon	Freehand Polygon	Drawing
Filled Oval	Oval	Drawing
Filled Polygon	Polygon	Drawing
Filled Rectangle	Rectangle	Drawing
Group	Ungroup	Drawing
Paste Format	Paste Values	Standard
Print	Print Preview	Standard
Run Macro	Step Macro	Macro
Sort Ascending	Sort Descending	Utility
Zoom In	Zoom Out	Utility

In this lesson, you learned about the tools contained in the Standard Toolbar, and about the eight other Toolbars. You learned how to customize your work area by repositioning and resizing the various Toolbars. In the next lesson, you will learn how to work with Excel's worksheets.

Lesson 5

Working with Worksheets

In this lesson you will learn how to open and save existing Excel worksheets. You will also learn how to create new worksheets.

Saving a Worksheet

It is important to always save your data. Saving your worksheet before leaving Excel should become part of your working routine.

To save a worksheet:

1. Pull down the File menu.

2. Select the Save command; the dialog box shown in Figure 5.1 appears. (This dialog box only appears the first time you save a file.)

3. If this is a new worksheet, enter the name of the file in the File Name text box. You may use any combination of letters or numbers up to eight characters (no spaces), such as 1992BDGT. Excel automatically adds .XLS to the file name as an extension. The full file name is then 1992BDGT.XLS.

4. Click on OK or press Enter.

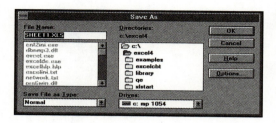

Figure 5.1   The File Save As dialog box.

Make a Mistake?   Click on Cancel anytime before step 4 to cancel the File **S**ave operation. If
you've already saved the file, but you typed something wrong, save it again. Be sure to delete the
unwanted copy after your work session.

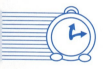

Save It Again   If you saved the file previously,
and you simply want to save the file and then
continue working, use the keyboard shortcut for
saving a file: Shift-F12. To do this, hold the Shift
key down as you press F12, then release. Your file
is now saved.

Saving a File with a New Name

You may want to save an existing worksheet with a different name, or in a different directory. You can do both of
these things and more by using the Save **A**s command:

1. Pull down the File menu.

2. Select the Save As command. The dialog box shown in Figure 5.1 will appear.

3. If you wish to save the worksheet under a new name (you will then have two copies—the original, and this one), type the new file name over the existing name in the File Name text box.

4. To save the file to a different directory, double-click on that directory in the Directories list box. The directory shown below Directories will change.

5. To save the file on a different drive, activate the Drives drop-down list box by clicking on the arrow on the right of the list. A list of available drives will appear. Click on the drive you wish to save to.

6. To save the file in a different format, activate the Save File as Type drop-down list box by clicking on the arrow on the right of the list. A list of formats will appear. You can choose to save your file in Lotus, dBASE, and text format, among others.

7. Click on OK or press Enter.

Excel 4.0 offers you an even faster alternative for saving your document. Simply click on the Save File tool in the Standard Toolbar.

A Little Insurance Before making major changes to any document, it is a good idea to always save it first. That way, if something goes wrong with a new procedure, you can simply reopen the saved file.

Opening a New Worksheet

To open a new worksheet, follow these steps:

1. Pull down the File menu.

2. Select New; the dialog box shown in Figure 5.2 appears.

3. Choose Worksheet.

4. Click on OK or press Enter. A new worksheet opens on-screen with a default name in the title bar. Excel numbers the files sequentially. For example, if you already have Sheet1 open, your screen will read Sheet2.

Figure 5.2 The New File dialog box.

 Excel 4.0 provides you with a shortcut for opening a new file. Simply click on the New Worksheet tool on the Standard Toolbar.

Opening an Existing Worksheet

To open an existing worksheet, follow these steps:

1. Pull down the File menu.

2. Select Open; the dialog box shown in Figure 5.3 appears.

3. If the file is not in the current directory, select the Directories list box. Then select the directory you wish to change to.

4. If the file is not on the current drive, select the Drives list box. Then select the drive you wish to change to.

5. Choose the file you wish to open from the File Name box.

6. Click on OK or press Enter.

Figure 5.3   The Open dialog box.

Excel 4.0 provides you with a shortcut for opening a file. Simply click on the Open File tool on the Standard Toolbar.

Navigating a Worksheet

You can move around an Excel worksheet by using the mouse or the keyboard, whichever is more convenient.

The Active Cell   The cell which will receive input or be affected by any formatting commands is the active cell. The active cell or cells are surrounded by a dark line.

To move the active cell a short distance:

- Use any of the arrow keys. For example, to move down one row, press ↓.

- Click on any cell with the mouse.

Using the scroll bars located on the bottom and right sides of the worksheet (see Lesson 2) is one of the easiest ways to move quickly around a large worksheet.

To scroll through one column, click on the right arrow located on the horizontal scroll bar.

To scroll through one row, click on the down arrow located on the vertical scroll bar.

To scroll one screen up or down, click between the arrows on the vertical scroll bar.

To scroll one screen left or right, click between the arrows on the horizontal scroll bar.

Going Somewhere?   To scroll to a general location in the worksheet, drag the scroll box to the appropriate place within the scroll bar.

To use the keyboard to move around the worksheet, use one of the key combinations from Table 5.1:

Table 5.1   Worksheet Navigation Keys

Key	Function
↑	Move one cell up
↓	Move one cell down
← or Shift-Tab	Move one cell left
→ or Tab	Move one cell right
PgUp	Move one screen up
PgDn	Move one screen down
Ctrl-PgUp	Move one screen left
Ctrl-PgDn	Move one screen right
End-any arrow key	Move in the indicated direction, to the last cell with data
Ctrl-End	Move to the last cell in the worksheet
Ctrl-Home	Move to the first cell in the worksheet (A1)

When You Know Where You're Going   You can move to a specific cell in the worksheet by selecting the Goto command on the Formula menu. In the **R**eference box, type the name of the cell you would like to move to (for example, type G12), and then click on OK or press Enter.

Moving Between Open Worksheets

Sometimes you may have more than one worksheet open at a time. There are many ways to move between open worksheets:

The Active Window   If you have more than one worksheet open, only one of them is considered active—the worksheet where the cell selector is located. The title bar of the active worksheet will be darker than the title bars of other open worksheets.

If the worksheet you would like to move to is visible:

• Click on any part of that worksheet to make it active.

If the worksheet you would like to move to is not visible:

1. Pull down the Window menu. A list of open worksheets will appear at the bottom of the menu.

2. Select the worksheet you wish to move to.

Make Some Room   You can temporarily move an open worksheet out of the way by reducing it to an icon at the bottom of the work area (see Lesson 2). Simply click on the Minimize button to minimize the worksheet. To restore the worksheet to its previous size, double-click on its icon.

Closing Worksheets

Closing a worksheet removes it from the screen. To close a worksheet:

1. Make the window you want to close active.

2. Pull down the File menu.

3. Choose Close.

4. If you have not yet saved the Worksheet, you will be prompted to do so.

In a Hurry? To quickly close a worksheet, double-click on the control button located in the upper left corner.

Save, Save, Save To avoid losing data, always save your worksheet files before closing them.

In this lesson, you learned how to open, close, and save worksheets. You also learned the basics for navigating a worksheet. The next lesson teaches you how to use Excel's workbooks.

Lesson 6

Using Excel's Workbooks

This lesson teaches you how to use workbooks to organize your files.

Beginning with Excel 4.0, you can save multiple worksheets in a workbook.

A Workbook A collection of worksheets, charts, and related information is called a workbook. Using workbooks is an easy way to keep all of the material for a related task together.

Building a Workbook

You start a workbook by first creating the workbook as if you were creating a file. You then add worksheet files to the workbook. To create a workbook:

1. Pull down the File menu.

2. Choose New.

3. In the New list box, choose Workbook.

4. Click on OK or press Enter. Your window should look similar to Figure 6.1.

Elements in workbook

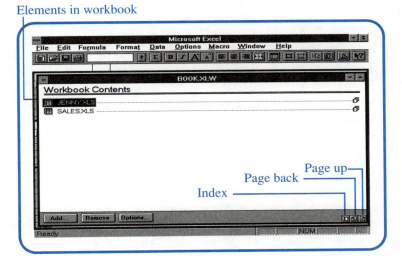

Figure 6.1   An Excel Workbook.

You can add worksheets to a workbook, including new or unopened worksheets. To add worksheets to a workbook (when the workbook window is visible):

1. Click on Add.

2. From the Add to Workbook dialog box, select a worksheet to add from the list. (This step is necessary only when you're adding an existing, open workbook.)

3. Click on Add, New, or Open. (If you select New, the New dialog box appears so that you can specify what kind of document to add. Selecting Open displays the Open dialog box so that you can select which worksheet to add.)

41

4. Repeat steps 1-3 until all the documents you want have been added to the workbook.

5. Click on Close.

Navigating Between Documents in a Workbook

There are many ways to navigate between documents in a workbook:

- From the workbook window, double-click on the documents you would like to switch to.

- At the bottom of a document or workbook window, activate the Shortcut menu by clicking on the Contents icon. Then select a document from the list.

- At the bottom of a document or workbook window, click on the Left Paging or Right Paging icon to move forward or backward one document in the workbook list.

Saving Documents in a Workbook

To save all the documents in a workbook:

1. Pull down the File menu.

2. Select Save Workbook.

3. If you wish to save the workbook under a new name (you will then have two copies—the original, and this one), simply type the new file name over the existing

one in the File **Name** text box. Excel will automatically add the .XLS extension.

4. To save the workbook in a different directory, double-click on that directory in the **Directories** list box. The directory shown above **Directories** will change.

5. To save the workbook on a different drive, activate the Drives drop-down list box by clicking on the arrow on the right of the list. A list of available drives will appear. Click on the drive you wish to save to.

6. Click on OK or press Enter.

In this lesson, you learned how to use workbooks. The next lesson teaches you how to enter data in Excel.

Entering and Editing Data

In this lesson, you will learn how to enter different types of data in an Excel worksheet.

Types of Data

There are many types of data that you can enter into an Excel worksheet. These include:

- Text

- Numbers

- Dates

- Times

- Formulas

As you enter data into a cell, it appears in that cell and also in the formula bar, as shown in Figure 7.1.

Cell Reference   Cancel Enter   Formula bar   Fill handle

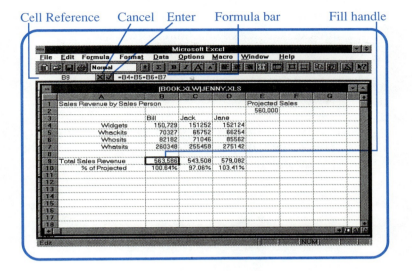

Figure 7.1   Data that you enter also appears in the formula bar.

Entering Text

Any combination of letters or numbers can be entered as text. Text is automatically left-aligned.

To enter text into a cell:

1. Select the cell into which you want to enter text.

2. Type the text.

3. Click on the Enter button on the formula bar or press Enter.

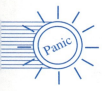

Bail out! To cancel an entry before you are done, click on the Cancel button or press Esc.

Number Text You may want to enter a number as text (for example, a zip code). Precede your entry with a single quotation mark ('), as in `'46220`. The quotation mark is an alignment prefix that tells Excel to treat the following characters as text and left-align them in the cell.

Entering Numbers

Valid numbers can include the numeric characters 0–9 and any of these special characters: + – ( ) , $ % . E e. Numbers are automatically right-aligned.

As you can see, you can include commas, decimal points, scientific notation (E and e), dollar signs, percentage signs, and parentheses in the values that you enter.

Although you can include punctuation, you may not want to. For example, rather than type a column of a hundred dollar amounts including the dollar signs and decimal points, you can type numbers such as `700` and `81.2`, and then format the column with dollar-sign formatting. Excel changes your entries to $700.00 and $81.20, respectively. Refer to Lesson 14 for more information.

To enter a number:

1. Select the cell into which you want to enter a number.

2. Type the number. To enter a negative number, precede it with a minus sign, or surround it with parentheses.

3. Click on the Enter button on the formula bar or press Enter.

Entering Dates and Times

Dates and times can be entered in a variety of formats. When you enter a date using a format shown in Table 7.1, Excel converts the date into a number which represents the number of days since January 1, 1900. This number is used whenever a calculation involves a date. Because a date is actually a number, when a date is entered correctly, it is right-aligned in the cell. You cannot perform calculations on a date that has not been entered correctly. If you enter a two-digit month, such as 04/08/58, it is truncated to one digit, 4/8/58.

Table 7.1 Valid Formats for Dates and Times

Format	Example
MM/DD/YY	4/8/58 or 04/08/58
MMM-YY	Jan-92
DD-MMM-YY	28-Oct-91
DD-MMM	6-Sep
HH:MM	16:50
HH:MM:SS	8:22:59
HH:MM AM/PM	7:45 PM
HH:MM:SS AM/PM	11:45:16 AM
MM/DD/YY HH:MM	11/8/80 4:20
HH:MM MM/DD/YY	4:20 11/18/80

To enter a date or time:

1. Select the cell into which you want to enter a date or time.

2. Type the date or time in the format in which you want it displayed.

3. Click on the Enter button on the formula bar or press Enter.

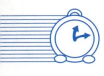

To Dash or To Slash   You can use dashes (-) or slashes (/) when typing dates. Capitalization is not important, since it is ignored. For example, 21 FEB becomes 21-Feb. By the way, FEB 21 also becomes 21-Feb.

Day or Night?   Unless you type AM or PM, Excel assumes that you are using a 24-hour military clock. Therefore, 8:20 is assumed to be AM, not PM, unless you type 8:20 PM.

Using Autofill

Excel 4.0 has a new tool that is designed to save you time in entering data in a series. A series is a collection of data with a logical progression, such as 1, 2, 3 or Qtr 1, Qtr 2, and Qtr 3.

Excel recognizes four types of series, shown in Table 7.2

Table 7.2 Data Series

Series	Initial Entry	Resulting Series
Linear	1,2	3,4,5
	100,99	98,97,96
	1,3	5,7,9
Growth	10 (step 5)	15,20,25
	10 (step 10)	20,30,40
Date	Mon	Tue, Wed, Thur
	Feb	Mar, Apr, May
	Qtr1	Qtr2, Qtr3, Qtr4
	1992	1993, 1994, 1995
Autofill	Team 1	Team 2, Team 3, Team 4
	Qtr 4	Qtr 1, Qtr 2, Qtr 3
	1st Quarter	2nd Quarter, 3rd Quarter, 4th Quarter

To create a series using Autofill by dragging:

1. Enter the first two values in a series.

2. Select the two cells.

3. Drag the series to adjacent cells by dragging the fill handle located at the lower right corner of the selected cells (see Figure 7.1).

4. Release the mouse button, and Excel fills the cells with values based on the initial values.

To create a series using Autofill with the Series command:

1. Enter a value in one cell.

2. Select the cells into which you want to extend the series.

3. Pull down the Data menu.

4. Choose Series. The dialog box shown in Figure 7.2 appears.

Figure 7.2 The Data Series dialog box.

5. Under Series, select Rows or Columns.

6. Under Type, choose a series type.

7. Adjust the Step value (amount between each series value), and Stop value (last value you want Excel to enter) if necessary.

8. Click on OK or press Enter, and the series is created.

Editing Data

After you have entered data into a cell, you may change it by editing.

To edit data in a cell:

1. Select the cell in which you want to edit data.

2. Position the cursor in the formula bar with the mouse, or press F2 to enter Edit mode.

3. Use the Backspace key to delete characters to the left of the cursor, or the Delete key to delete characters to the right of the cursor. Type any additional characters. They will be added to the left of the cursor.

4. Click on the Enter button on the formula bar or press Enter to accept your changes.

Stop the Edit   To cancel changes to a cell before you are done, click on the Cancel button or press Esc.

Using Undo

There is an easy way to undo the last change that you made to the worksheet. To undo a change:

1. Pull down the Edit menu.

2. Choose Undo Typing.

The actual command shown in step 2 will vary, depending on what you are trying to undo. For example, the Edit menu might display **Undo Formatting**, **Undo Sorting**, or **Undo Alignment**.

Act Fast To Undo a Change   You will not be able to undo a change after you have changed something else. If you are not able to undo a change, Can't Undo will be displayed on the Edit menu.

To undo an Undo (reverse a change):

1. Pull down the Edit menu.

2. Choose Redo.

Like the Undo command, the Redo command will also vary, depending on what you are trying to redo. For example, the Edit menu might display Redo Formatting, Redo Sorting, or Redo Alignment.

Undo It Easier   To quickly undo a change, press Ctrl-Z, or click on the Undo tool on the Utility Toolbar if you have that Toolbar displayed.

In this lesson you learned how to enter different types of data, and how to make changes and undo those changes.

Lesson 8
Working with Ranges

In this lesson, you will learn how to select and name cell ranges.

What Is a Range?

A range is a rectangular group of connected cells. The cells in a range may all be in a column, or a row, or any combination of columns and rows, as long as the range forms a rectangle, as shown in Figure 8.1.

Learning how to use ranges can save you time. For example, you can select a range and use it to format a group of cells with one step. You can use a range to print only a selected group of cells. You can also use ranges in formulas.

Ranges are referred to by their anchor points (the top left corner and the lower right corner). For example, the ranges shown in Figure 8.1 are B4:D7, A9:D9, and F2.

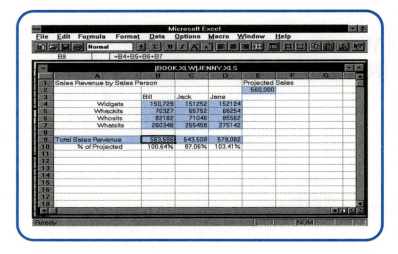

Figure 8.1 A range is any combination of cells that forms a rectangle.

Selecting a Range

To select a range, use the mouse:

1. Move the mouse pointer to the upper left corner of a range.

2. Click and hold the left mouse button.

3. Drag the mouse to the lower right corner of the range.

4. Release the mouse button. The selected range will be highlighted.

Sorry, Wrong Range   If you accidently select the wrong range, simply reselect it with the mouse.

A Quick Selection   To quickly select a row or a column, click on the row or column name at the edge of the worksheet.

Select the Whole Thing   To select the entire worksheet, click on the rectangle above row 1 and left of column A.

Naming a Cell Range

Sometimes, when working with a lot of data, it is more convenient to name parts of that data to use in formulas and to manipulate that data by sorting and such. Once a range is named, you can use that name (instead of the name of the cell locations) to refer to that data. For example, you could give a column which holds data for January the range name JAN.

To name a cell range:

1. Select the range of cells to be named.

2. Pull down the Formula menu.

3. Choose Define Name. The dialog box shown in Figure 8.2 appears.

Figure 8.2   The Define Name dialog box.

4. You may accept the name that Excel provides (if any), or type in a new one in the **Name** text box. Valid names can include letters, numbers, - \ . or ?. Range names must begin with a letter, the minus sign, or the back slash (\).

5. Click on OK or press Enter.

Name a Range Fast   To quickly name a range, select the range to be named and press Ctrl-F3.

   In this lesson, you learned how to select and name ranges. In the next lesson, you will learn how to copy, move, and erase data.

Lesson 9
Copying, Moving, and Erasing Data

In this lesson, you will learn to organize your worksheet to meet your changing needs by copying, moving and erasing data.

When you copy or move data, a copy of that data is placed in a temporary storage area called the clipboard.

What Is the Clipboard?   The clipboard is an area of memory that is accessible to all Windows programs. The clipboard is used by all Windows programs to copy or move data from place to place within a program, or between programs. The techniques that you learn here are the same ones used in all Windows programs.

Copying Data

You make copies of data to use in other sections of your worksheet. The data that you copy remains in place, and a copy of it is placed where you indicate.

To copy data:

1. Select the range or cell that you wish to copy.

2. Pull down the Edit menu.

3. Choose Copy.

4. Move the cursor to the first cell in the area where you would like to place the copy. To copy the data to another worksheet, change to that worksheet.

5. Pull down the Edit menu.

6. Choose Paste, and the data is copied.

Quick Copying To copy data quickly, select the data to be copied and press Ctrl-Insert or Ctrl-C. This copies the data to the clipboard. To paste, simply press Enter, or Ctrl-V.

Excel 4.0 offers you a fast way to copy—Drag and Drop. To use Drag and Drop, you use the fill handle, a small square located in the lower right corner of a selected cell. (If the fill handle doesn't appear, select Options Workspace, and then turn on the Cell Drag and Drop option.) Simply drag the fill handle to select the cells to which you wish to copy data. You can also copy by using tools. The Copy tool is located on the Utility Toolbar. You can also customize any Toolbar by adding the Fill Right, Fill Down, Cut, and Paste tools from the Customize dialog box.

Multiple Copies You can copy the same data to several places in the worksheet by repeating the Edit Paste command. Data copied to the clipboard remains there until it's replaced by something else.

Moving Data

Moving data is similar to copying, except that the data is cut from its original place and moved to the new location.

To move data:

1. Select the range or cell that you wish to move.

2. Pull down the Edit menu.

3. Choose Cut.

4. Move the cursor to the first cell in the area where you would like to place the data. To move the data to another worksheet, simply change to that worksheet.

5. Pull down the Edit menu.

6. Choose Paste, and the data is moved.

Move It!   To move data quickly, select the data to be moved and press Shift-Delete or Ctrl-X. This moves the data to the clipboard. To paste, simply press Enter or Ctrl-V.

With Excel 4.0, you can use the Shortcut menu to save time when copying or moving data. Select the data to be copied or moved and click the right mouse button to open the Shortcut menu; then choose the appropriate command—Cut, Copy, or Paste. You can also move data to another location with Drag and Drop. Select the cells you want to move. Point to the border around them so that the mouse pointer changes from a plus to an arrow. Drag the border to a new location and release the mouse button.

Watch Out! When copying or moving data, be careful when you indicate the range where the data should be pasted. Excel will paste the data over any existing data in the indicated range.

Erasing Data

When erasing data from your worksheet, Excel gives you a lot of options. You can completely remove the data, or simply remove the cell's formatting, formulas, or attached notes.

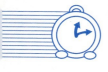

Remove All Data To completely remove data from a cell, use the Edit Clear command. The contents of the cell will be removed, but the surrounding cells will not be affected. When you use the Delete command, the cell is removed, and the data in surrounding cells is moved on top of it. You will learn more about the **D**elete command in the next lesson.

Using the Edit Clear Command

Use the **E**dit Clear command to remove all or part of the contents of a cell, without affecting the position of the surrounding cells. With the Clear command, you can remove the data from a cell, or just its formula, formatting, or attached notes.

To clear cells:

1. Select the range of cells you wish to clear.

2. Pull down the Edit menu.

3. Choose Clear. The Clear dialog box shown in Figure 9.1 appears.

Figure 9.1 The Clear dialog box.

4. Click on the option you would like to use: Clear All, Clear Formats, Clear Formulas, or Clear Notes.

5. Click on OK or press Enter.

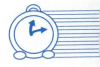

A Clean Slate To clear data quickly, select the range of cells to be cleared and press the Delete key. To clear formulas only, press Ctrl-Delete.

Excel 4.0 offers you another alternative to clear data—the Shortcut menu. Select the range of cells to be cleared and press the right mouse button to open the Shortcut menu. Choose Clear from the menu.

In this lesson, you learned how to copy and move data. You also learned how to clear data from cells. In the next lesson, you will learn how to delete and insert cells, rows, and columns.

Inserting and Deleting Cells, Rows, and Columns

In this lesson, you will learn how to rearrange your worksheet by adding and deleting cells, rows, and columns.

Inserting Individual Cells

Sometimes you will need to insert information into a worksheet, right in the middle of existing data. With the Insert command, you can insert a single cell, or whole rows and columns.

Confused?   Inserting cells in the middle of existing data will cause those other cells to be shifted down a row or over a column. Exercise caution when inserting cells.

To insert a single cell or a group of cells:

1. Move your pointer to the place where you would like the new cell inserted or select the range where you want to insert new cells.

2. Pull down the Edit menu.

3. Choose Insert. The Insert dialog box shown in Figure 10.1 appears.

Figure 10.1   The Insert dialog box.

4. Select Shift Cells **R**ight or Shift Cells **D**own.

5. Click on OK or press Enter. Excel inserts the cell and shifts the data in the other cells in the indicated direction.

Inserting Rows and Columns

Inserting entire rows and columns in your worksheet is similar to inserting a single cell.

To insert a row or column:

1. Move your pointer to the place where you would like the new row or column inserted.

2. Pull down the Edit menu.

3. Choose Insert. The Insert dialog box appears.

4. Select Entire **R**ow or Entire Column.

5. Click on OK or press Enter. Excel inserts the row or column and shifts the data in the other cells in the appropriate direction. Figure 10.2 simulates a worksheet before and after a row is inserted.

Insert Rows or Columns Quickly To insert rows or columns without displaying the dialog box, click on the letter or number, and then choose Edit Insert. You can also select multiple rows or columns to insert multiple rows or columns.

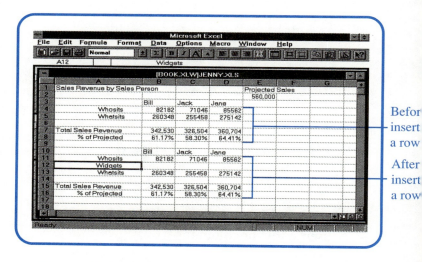

Befor insert a row

After insert a row

Figure 10.2 Inserting a row in a worksheet.

Excel 4.0 offers you several ways to insert data, and the Shortcut menu is one. Select the row or column where you would like to insert data, and press the right mouse button to open the Shortcut menu. Choose Insert from the menu. There are also three tools you can add to any Toolbar from the Customize dialog box—the Insert tool, Insert Column tool, and the Insert Row tool.

Deleting Individual Cells or Cell Ranges

Deleting cells is the opposite of inserting them. When you use the Delete command, the data in the surrounding cells moves up a row or over a column, covering the data in the cells you delete. So, you delete cells by moving data on top of the cells to delete.

To delete a single cell or cell range:

1. Select the cell or range of cells you wish to delete.

2. Pull down the Edit menu.

3. Choose Delete. The Delete dialog box shown in Figure 10.3 appears.

Figure 10.3   The Delete dialog box.

4. Click on Shift Cells Left or Shift Cells Up.

5. Click on OK or press Enter.

Deleting Rows and Columns

Deleting rows and columns is similar to deleting a single cell.

To delete a row or column:

1. Select the row or column you wish to delete.

2. Pull down the Edit menu.

3. Choose Delete. The Delete dialog box appears.

4. Click on Entire **R**ow or Entire **C**olumn.

5. Click on OK or press Enter. Excel deletes the row or column and shifts the data in the other cells in the appropriate direction. Figure 10.4 simulates a worksheet before and after a row was deleted.

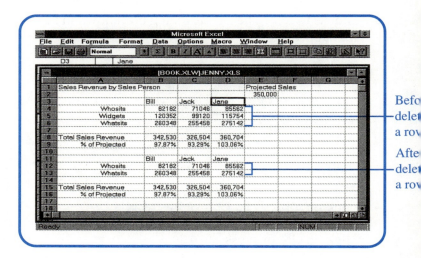

Befo
delet
a rov

Afte
delet
a rov

Figure 10.4   Deleting a row in a worksheet. Sorry, Charlie!

Excel 4.0 offers you several ways to delete data, and one is using the Shortcut menu. Select the range of cells to be deleted, and press the right mouse button to open the Shortcut menu. Choose Delete from the menu. There are also three tools that you can add to any Toolbar from the Customize dialog box—the Delete tool, the Delete Column tool, and the Delete Row tool.

In this lesson, you learned how to insert and delete rows and columns. In the next lesson, you will learn how to use formulas.

Writing Formulas

In this lesson, you will learn how to use formulas to calculate results in your worksheets.

What Is a Formula?

A formula is a mathematical expression which calculates a result.

What is a Formula? A formula defines the relationship between two or more values. Formulas include references to the values in other cells, and formulas manipulate these values to produce results.

Formulas consist of numbers, mathematical operators, and references to other cells.

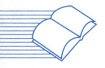

Cell References Expressions which reference the data stored in other cells are called *cell references*. A cell reference is written with the column reference first, followed by the row reference. For example, a cell in column E, row 4 is referred to as E4. When the pointer is in a particular cell, you see the cell reference in the reference area of the formula bar.

Entering Formulas

To enter a formula, you must include:

The equal sign (=)   All formulas must begin with an equal sign. This is how Excel identifies the expression as a formula.

A cell reference   You may of course include multiple cell references, in order to manipulate the values of several cells.

You also may include:

Numbers   For example, you could take the contents of cell B5 and divide it by the number 12 to get a monthly total.

Mathematical Operators   A mathematical operator (such as + or −) is needed if your formula contains more than one cell reference or number.

Function   A function performs a specific task, such as adding a group of numbers to compute a sum.

Range Reference   When using functions, you may use range references, such as A2:E2, in order to write a formula which references the values of several adjoining cells.

Range Names   You can use range names in place of range references in formulas.

You will learn more about functions and range references in the next lesson.

Writing a formula is like writing a mathematical expression. Formulas use the following mathematical operators, shown in Table 11.1:

Table 11.1 Mathematical Operators Used in Excel Formulas

Operator	Meaning	Example	Result
+	Addition	4+2	6
–	Subtraction	4-2	2
*	Multiplication	4*2	8
/	Division	4/2	2
^	Exponentiation	4^2	16

The following are example Excel formulas:

=J8	This will place the value of cell J8 in the cell containing the formula. When the value in J8 changes, this cell will change too.
=J8/12	Divides the value of cell J8 by 12.
=J8+A5	Adds the values of cells J8 and A5.
=(A5+J8)/4	Divides the total of cells A5 and J8 by 4
=J8*10%	Multiplies the value of cell J8 by 10%

70

To enter a formula:

1. Move the pointer to the cell where the formula will reside.

2. Type the equal sign (=).

3. Type the formula. The formula appears in the formula bar.

4. Press Enter, and the result is calculated.

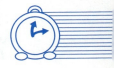

Quick Cell References   You can use the mouse when typing cell references. Just click on the cell that you want to reference in a formula, and the name of that cell appears in the formula at that point.

Error!   Make sure that you did not commit one of these common errors: trying to divide by zero or a blank cell, referring to a blank cell, deleting a cell being used in a formula, or using a range name when a single cell name is expected.

Operator Precedence

When typing your formula in Excel, it is important to remember operator precedence.

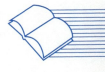

Operator Precedence   The order in which a formula will be evaluated, based on the mathematical operators being used, is known as *operator precedence*.

Any formula which involves more than one mathematical operator will be calculated in steps. The order that the steps are calculated in is based on the mathematical operator involved. This is the order of precedence for mathematical operators in Excel:

%	Percentage
^	Exponentiation
* and /	Multiplication and Division
+ and −	Addition and Subtraction

For example, if you typed the following formulas, you would get these results:

Formula	Result	Order of Calculation
8-3*2	2	$3 * 2 = 6, 8 - 6 = 2$
(8-3)*2	10	$8 - 3 = 5, 5 * 2 = 10$

Displaying Formulas

Sometimes when you are working in a complex worksheet, it's nice to be able to verify the formulas involved. Moving from cell to cell in order to see the formula displayed in the formula bar can be time-consuming. Excel offers you an alternative.

To display formulas (instead of their results):

1. Pull down the Options menu.

2. Choose Display. The Display Options dialog box shown in Figure 11.1 appears.

Figure 11.1   The Display Options dialog box.

3. Click on the Formulas check box. An x appears, indicating that the option has been turned on.

4. Click on OK or press Enter.

Display Formulas Quickly   Use the keyboard shortcut, Ctrl-', to display formulas. Hold down the Ctrl key, and press the apostrophe (').

Editing Formulas

Editing formulas is the same as editing any entry in Excel.

To edit a formula:

1. Select the formula you want to edit.

2. Position the cursor in the formula bar, or press F2 to enter Edit mode.

3. Use the Backspace key to delete characters to the left of the cursor or the Delete key to delete characters to the right of the cursor. Type any additional characters. They will be added to the right of the cursor.

4. Click on the Enter button on the formula bar or press Enter.

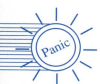

Change Your Mind? To cancel changes to a cell before you are done, click on the Cancel button or press Esc.

Copying Formulas

Copying formulas is similar to copying other data in a worksheet. To copy formulas:

1. Select the formula that you wish to copy.

2. Pull down the Edit menu.

3. Choose Copy.

4. Move the cursor to the first cell in the area where you would like to place the copy. To copy data to another worksheet, change to that worksheet.

5. Pull down the Edit menu.

6. Choose Paste, and the data is copied.

To copy formulas quickly, try using the Drag and Drop fill handle. The fill handle is a small square that appears in the lower right corner when a cell is selected. Drag the fill handle to select the cells into which you wish to copy the formula. You may also use the Fill Down or Fill Right tools from the Customize dialog box. You can also copy with the Copy tool located on the Utility Toolbar. In addition, you can customize any Toolbar by adding the Cut and Paste tools from the Customize dialog box.

Keyboard Shortcuts If you prefer a more conventional method, try the keyboard shortcuts to copy formulas: select the formula to be copied, and press Ctrl-Insert or Ctrl-C. This copies the data to the clipboard. To paste, simply press Enter, or Ctrl-V.

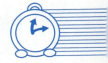

Get an Error? If you get an error after copying a formula, verify the cell references in the copied formula. See "Using Relative and Absolute Cell Addressing" for more details.

Using Relative and Absolute Cell Addressing

When you copy a formula from one place in the worksheet to another, the cells that are referenced in the formula are adjusted to compensate for the movement.

Suppose you had a formula that added four cells together from column B to achieve a total. You want to use this same basic formula over and over in several columns. The formula would have to be adjusted to reference the four cells in the new column, C, not the original cells. Excel does this "adjusting" for you, as shown in Figure 11.2.

Cell references are adjusted for Column C

Figure 11.2   Excel adjusts cell references when copying formulas.

Sometimes, you do not want the cell references to be adjusted when formulas are copied. That's when absolute references become important.

Absolute vs. Relative   An *absolute reference* is a cell reference in a formula that does not change when copied to a new location. A *relative reference* is a cell reference in a formula which is adjusted when the formula is copied.

In Figure 11.2, the formula B4+B5+B6+B7 in cell B9 uses relative references. When the formula was copied from cell

B9 to C9, its cell references were adjusted and the formula became C4+C5+C6+C7.

The formula in cells B10, C10, and D10 uses an absolute reference to cell F2, which holds the projected sales for this year. (B10, C10, and D10 divide the sums from row 9 of each column by the contents of cell F2.) If you didn't use an absolute reference, when you copied the formula from B10 to C10, the cell reference would be incorrect.

Some formulas use mixed references. For example, if you had the formula $A2/2 in cell C2, and you copied that formula to cell D10, the result would be the formula $A10/2. The row reference would be adjusted, but not the column. Using relative cell referencing as in the formula A2/2, when copied to cell D10, the result would be the formula B10/2.

Mixed References   A reference which is only partially absolute, such as A$2, or $A2 is called a *mixed reference*. When a formula which uses a mixed reference is copied to another cell, only part of the cell reference is adjusted.

In this lesson, you learned how to enter and edit formulas. You also learned when to use relative and absolute cell addressing. In the next lesson, you will learn how to use Excel's built-in functions in formulas.

Lesson 12
Using Built-In Functions

In this lesson you will learn how to create complex formulas with Excel's built-in functions.

What Are Built-In Functions?

Functions help to simplify complex formulas. They are built-in formulas provided by Excel. For example, instead of typing `=B1+B2+B3` to add three numbers, you can use a function (SUM) to total them. The SUM function is written `=SUM(B1:B3)`, which means you would have to write fewer numbers. Built-in functions can use range references such as B1:B3, or range names such as SALES.

There are many types of functions available—Mathematical functions, such as ROUND(); Statistical functions, such as AVERAGE(); Financial functions, such as FV(); and Date/Time functions, such as YEAR(). A listing of Excel functions can be found in the Table of Functions at the back of this book.

Using the AutoSum Tool

Since SUM is one of the most-used functions, Excel created a fast way to enter it. The AutoSum tool guesses what cells you want summed, based on where the cursor is when you activate AutoSum. If AutoSum selects an incorrect range of cells, you can edit the selection.

To use AutoSum:

1. Select a cell to hold the sum. You will have the best results if you choose a cell at the end of a row or column of data.

2. Click on the AutoSum tool on the Standard Toolbar.

3. If you need to adjust the range of cells that AutoSum has selected, edit the selection. You can also use the mouse or the cursor keys to adjust the range selection.

4. When the range is correct, click on the Enter box in the formula bar or press Enter. The total for the range selected is calculated.

Using Formula Paste Function

In order to enter formulas quickly and easily, use the Formula Paste Function command.

To enter a formula using the Paste command:

1. Move to the cell where you want to add a formula.

2. Pull down the Formula menu.

3. Choose Paste Function, and the dialog box shown in Figure 12.1 appears.

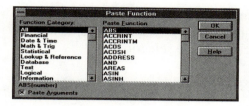

Figure 12.1   The Paste Function dialog box.

4. Select the function you want from the Paste **F**unction
list box. If you would like, you can narrow the display
of functions by selecting a category from the Function
Category list box. A sample of the function selected
appears just below the Function Category list box.

5. If you do not want the arguments pasted into the
formula bar along with the Function, deselect the Paste
Arguments check box.

In this lesson, you learned about Excel's built-in functions. You learned how to enter functions quickly with the
AutoSum tool and the Paste command.

Lesson 13

Printing Your Worksheet

In this lesson, you will learn all you need to print your worksheet.

Changing the Print Setup

Before you print, you must choose how you want your worksheet printed. Use the File Page Setup command to display a dialog box offering options that affect the appearance of the printed worksheet. The options you can select from include:

Orientation   Select from Portrait (8 1/2 by 11 inches, for example) or Landscape (11 by 8 1/2 inches, for example). The actual paper sizes are selected under Paper Size.

Paper Size   8 1/2 by 11 inches, by default. You can choose from other sizes.

Margins   You can adjust the size of the left, right, top, and bottom margins. You can also choose whether to center the data on the page horizontally or vertically.

Page Order   You can indicate how data in the worksheet should be read and printed: in sections from top to bottom or in sections from left to right.

Scaling   You can reduce and enlarge your worksheet or force it to fit within a specific page size.

Row or Column Heading   You can specify that row and column headings are printed.

Cell Gridlines   You can print the square lines around each cell.

Black and White Cells   You can print the color in the worksheet as patterns, or choose plain black and white.

Start Page No.'s At   You can set the starting page number to something other than 1.

Headers and Footers   You can add headers (such as a title which repeats at the top of each page) or footers (such as page numbers, which repeat at the bottom of each page).

To change the page setup:

1. Pull down the File menu.

2. Choose Page Setup. The dialog box shown in Figure 13.1 appears.

3. Choose the options you would like to use.

4. Click on OK or press Enter.

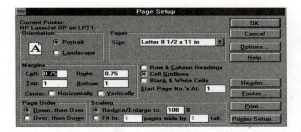

Figure 13.1   The Page Setup dialog box.

Choosing the Print Area

After selecting the options for the page setup, select the area of the worksheet that you wish to print. If you skip this step, Excel will print all the data in the worksheet.

To choose the print area:

1. Select the range of data you wish to print.

2. Pull down the Options menu.

3. Choose Set Print Area.

Printing Titles   You can print a title at the top of each page from data in the worksheet. Select the Options Set Print Titles command. If you choose this option, do not include these cells in the print range.

Excel 4.0 has a quick way to set the print area—the Print Area tool, located on the Utility Toolbar.

Adjusting Page Breaks

When you print a worksheet, Excel will determine the page breaks based on the page setup and the selected print area. You may want to override the automatic page breaks with your own breaks. Before you add page breaks, you may want to try these things:

- Adjust the widths of individual columns to make the best use of space.

- Consider printing the worksheet sideways (using Landscape orientation).

- Change the left, right, top, and bottom margins to smaller values.

If after trying these, you still want to insert page breaks, first determine whether you need to limit the number of columns on a page or to limit the number of rows on a page.

If you want to limit the number of columns:

1. Move your cursor to the column to the right of the last column you want on the page. For example, if you want Excel to print only columns A through G on the first page, move your cursor to column H, one column to the right of G.

2. Move to row one of that column.

3. Pull down the Options menu.

4. Choose Set Page Break.

5. A page break (dashed line) appears.

If you want to limit the number of rows:

1. Move your cursor to the row just below the last row you want on the page. For example, if you want Excel to print only rows 1 through 12 on the first page, move your cursor to row 13, which is one row below row 12.

2. Move to column A of that row.

3. Pull down the Options menu.

4. Choose Set Page Break.

5. A page break (dashed line) appears.

One Step Page Breaks You can set the lower right corner of a worksheet in one step. Move to the cell located below and to the right of the last cell for the page, and then select the Options Set Page Break command. For example, if you wanted cell G12 to be the last cell on that page, move to cell H13 and set the page break.

Make a Mistake? To remove a page break, move to the cell that you used to set the page break and select the Options Remove Page Break command. (To remove a vertical page break, place the cursor to the right of it. To remove a horizontal page break, place the cursor below it. The correct cell will be to the right and below the dotted lines which mark the page break.)

Previewing a Print Job

After you've determined your page setup, print area, and page breaks (if any), you can preview your print job before you print.

To preview a print job:

1. Pull down the File menu.

2. Choose Print Preview. Your worksheet appears as it will when printed, as shown in Figure 13.2.

A Close-Up View Zoom in on any area of the preview by clicking on it with the mouse. You can also use the Zoom button.

Printing

After setting the page setup and previewing your data, it is time to print.

Lets you move between pages   Closes the preview window

Zooms in on part of the display

Prints the worksheet

Lets you adjust settings

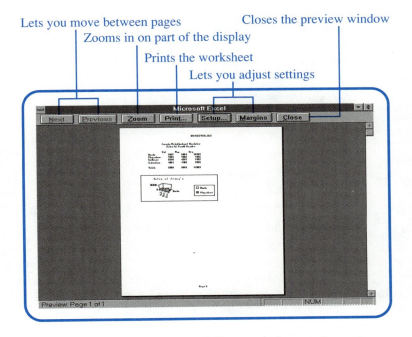

Figure 13.2   Your worksheet can be previewed before it is printed.

To print your worksheet:

1. Pull down the File menu.

2. Choose Print, and the dialog box shown in Figure 13.3 appears.

3. Select the options you would like to use.

4. Click on OK or press Enter.

Quick-Change Artist   To reach the Print dialog box quickly, press the keyboard shortcut, Ctrl-Shift-F12.

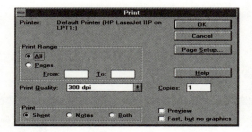

Figure 13.3 The Print dialog box.

Excel 4.0 offers you a quick method to print—the Print tool located on the Standard Toolbar.

In this lesson, you learned how to print your worksheet. In the next lesson, you will learn how to customize the formatting of numbers and text.

Lesson 14

Adjusting Number Formats and Alignment

In this lesson, you will learn how to customize the appearance of numbers in your worksheet.

Numeric Display Formats

In Lesson 6, "Entering and Editing Data," you learned about the many formats for dates and times in Excel. Excel also offers you a variety of numeric formats from which to choose, as shown in Table 14.1:

Table 14.1   Excel's Numeric Formats

Number Format	Display when you enter:			
	2000	**2**	**-2**	**.2**
General	2000	2	-2	.2
0	2000	2	-2	0
0.00	2000.00	2.00	-2.00	.20
#,##0	2,000	2	-2	0
#,##0.00	2,000.00	2.00	-2.00	.20
$#,##0_); ($#,##0)	$2,000	$2	($2)	$0

continues

89

Table 14.1 Continued

Number Format	Display when you enter:			
$#,##0.00_); ($#,##0.00)	$2,000.00	$2.00	($2.00)	$0.20
0%	2000%	200%	-200%	20%
0.00%	2000.00%	200.00%	-200.00%	20.00%
0.00E+00	2.00E+03	2.00E+00	-2.00E+00	2.00E-01
#?/?	2000	2	-1	1/5

Changing the Display Format

After deciding on a suitable numeric format, follow these steps:

1. Select the cell or range you wish to format.

2. Pull down the Format menu.

3. Choose Number, and the dialog box shown in Figure 14.1 appears.

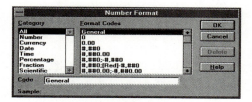

Figure 14.1 The Number Format dialog box.

4. Select the Category and Format Code you would like to use. A test result will display in the Sample box.

5. Click on OK or press Enter.

Pounding Headache? If a cell shows all pound signs (#######) after you apply a format, don't panic. Excel displays pound signs to let you know that the width of a cell is too small for a particular entry. See Lesson 17 to learn how to change column width.

The Formatting Toolbar There are many tools on the Formatting Toolbar you can use to quickly change number formats. Choose from the Currency, Percent, Comma, Increase Decimal Points, and Decrease Decimal Points tools. You can also change the Number format of a cell by using the Shortcut menu; press the right mouse button to display it.

Changing Alignments

When you enter data into an Excel worksheet, that data is aligned automatically. Text is aligned on the left, and numbers are aligned on the right.

Data can also be aligned vertically in a cell—at the top, at the bottom, or in the center of the cell. The default vertical alignment is bottom.

You can also rotate text (change its orientation) so that it reads sideways.

To change the alignment:

1. Select the cell or range you wish to align.

2. Pull down the Format menu.

3. Choose Alignment and the dialog box shown in Figure 14.2 appears.

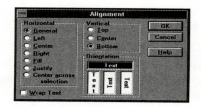

Figure 14.2 The Format Alignment dialog box.

4. Select the alignment you want.

5. Click on OK or press Enter.

An Alignment Shortcut Use the Shortcut menu to change the alignment of a cell or range quickly. Highlight the cell or range you wish to align and press the right mouse button to activate the Shortcut menu.

With Excel 4.0, you can also use the Left Align, Center Align, and Right Align tools on the Standard Toolbar to change alignment.

A Lot to Align? To repeat the alignment format command in another cell, use the **R**epeat Alignment command from the **E**dit menu. (The command appears as "**R**epeat Alignment" only after you have adjusted the alignment in a cell or range.)

Centering Text over Multiple Columns

You may want to center your entry not within a cell, but over several cells. For example, you might want to center a title over a section of your worksheet. Excel 4.0 has an added feature which makes this easy to do.

To center text over multiple columns:

1. Select the range which contains the text you want to center.

2. Pull down the Format menu.

3. Choose Alignment.

4. Choose Center Across Selection.

5. Click on OK or press Enter.

A Little Off-Center   If your entry is not centered correctly, make sure that you select the entire range in which the text should be centered. For example, to center the words 1991 Sales in cell C5 over three columns C, D, and E, select the range C5:E5.

Excel 4.0 offers you a fast way to center text—the Center Across Columns tool on the Standard Toolbar. You can also use the Shortcut menu to access the Alignment dialog box. Press the right mouse button to access the Shortcut menu.

Changing the Default Display Format and Alignment

When you enter the same type of data into a large worksheet, it is sometimes convenient to change the default format. You then can change the format for only those cells which are exceptions. Note that when you change the default, it affects all the cells in the worksheet.

You can change the default settings for number format, alignment, and others. To change the defaults:

1. Pull down the Format menu.

2. Choose Style. The Format Style dialog box appears.

3. In the Style Name list box, select Normal.

4. Click on the Define button, and the dialog box shown in Figure 14.3 appears.

5. Under Change, click on the Number check box to change the default format for numbers. Click on Alignment to change the default alignment for all cells. The appropriate dialog box appears.

6. Select the new default and click on OK or press Enter. You will be returned to the Format Style dialog box.

Figure 14.3   The Style dialog box.

7. Click on OK or press Enter.

In this lesson, you learned how to format numbers and align data to your preference. In the next lesson, you will learn how to format text.

Changing Text Attributes

In this lesson, you will learn how to change the appearance of text in your worksheet.

What Attributes Can You Change?

There are many textual attributes that you can change:

Style For example, Bold, Italic, Underline, and Strikeout.

Font For example, System, Roman, and MS Sans Serif.

Color For example, Red, Magenta, and Cyan.

 **What Is a Font?** *Font* refers to the combination of typeface, weight, and size. The size of a particular character is measured in *points*. (One point is equal to 1/72 of an inch.)

Figure 15.1 shows a worksheet after different attributes have been changed for selected text.

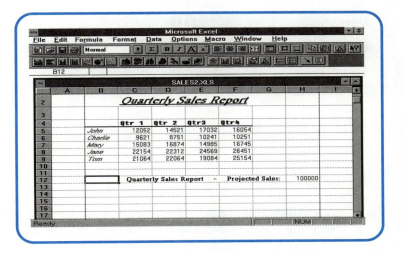

Figure 15.1   A sampling of several text attributes.

Using the Format Font Command

You use the Format Font command to change the attributes of text in your worksheet.

To use the Format Font command:

1. Select the cell or range which you want to format.

2. Pull down the Format menu.

3. Choose Font. The dialog box shown in Figure 15.2 appears.

4. Select the attributes you want to change.

5. Click on OK or press Enter.

97

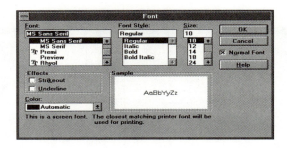

Figure 15.2   The Font dialog box.

Attribute Shortcuts   There are many keyboard shortcuts that you can use to quickly change text attributes. To change text to Normal, use Ctrl-1; for Bold, use Ctrl-B; for Italic, use Ctrl-I; for Underline, use Ctrl-U; and for Strikeout, use Ctrl-5.

Changing Text Attributes with Tools

Excel 4 offers many tools that you can use to quickly change text attributes. For example, the Standard Toolbar includes the Bold, Italic, Increase Font Size, and Decrease Font Size tools.

The Formatting Toolbar is also useful when changing text attributes. The Formatting Toolbar is shown in Figure 15.3.

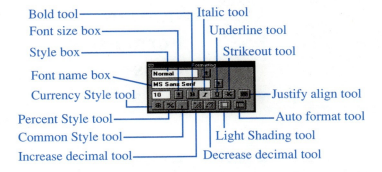

Figure 15.3 The Formatting Toolbar, moved and resized on the worksheet.

To use a tool to change text attributes:

1. Select the cell or range that you want to change.

2. Select the tool for the attribute you want to change, and the text changes.

Change Before You Type You can activate the attributes you want before you type text. For example, if you want a title in Bold, 12-point MS Sans Serif, set these attributes with the **Format Font** command, and then type the title.

In this lesson, you learned how to customize your text to achieve the look you want. In the next lesson, you will learn how to add borders and shading to your worksheet.

Lesson 16

Formatting Cells

In this lesson, you will learn how to add pizzazz to your worksheets by adding borders and shading.

Using the Format Borders Command

You can use borders and shading to highlight important information such as totals, comparison values, and so on. Used sparingly, borders and shading can add emphasis to your worksheet data. You can place a dark line (border) on any cell in the following areas:

Left, Right   Places the border on the left or right side of the cell or range.

Top, Bottom   Places the border on the top or bottom side of the cell or range.

Outline   Places the border around the edge of the cell or range.

A sample of several borders can be found in Figure 16.1.

Borders

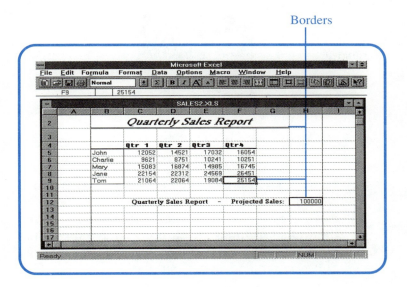

Figure 16.1   A sampling of borders.

To format the borders of a cell or range:

1. Select the cell or range to format.

2. Pull down the Format menu.

3. Choose Border. The dialog box shown in Figure 16.2 appears.

4. Select the border and style (thickness) you want.

5. Click on OK or press Enter.

Figure 16.2   The Border dialog box.

 **Hiding Gridlines**   When adding borders to a worksheet, hide the gridlines for better effect. Select the Options Display command. Clear the x from the Cells Gridlines check box. To avoid printing gridlines with your worksheet, select the File Page Setup command and clear the x from the Cell Gridlines checkbox.

 **Borders Everywhere**   Borders are shared by adjoining cells, so remember that placing a Top border on one cell is the same as placing a Bottom border on the cell above it.

 To add borders quickly, use the Outline and Bottom Border tools on the Standard Toolbar. You can also add Left, Right, Top, and Double Bottom tools from the Customize dialog box to any Toolbar. To access the Customize dialog box, use the Options Toolbars Customize command.

Using the Format Patterns Command

For a simple but dramatic effect, add shading to your worksheets. A sample worksheet is shown in Figure 16.3.

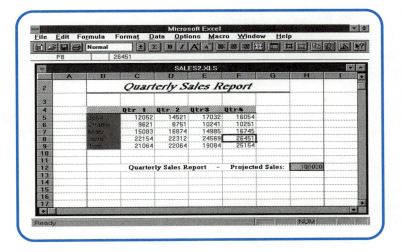

Figure 16.3   A worksheet with added shading.

To add shading to cell or range:

1. Select the cell or range you want to add shading too.

2. Pull down the Format menu.

3. Choose Pattern. The dialog box shown in Figure 16.4 appears.

Figure 16.4   Selecting a shading pattern.

4. Select the shading pattern you would like to use. You can also select a **F**oreground or **B**ackground color. A preview of the result is displayed in the Sample box.

103

5. Click on OK or press Enter.

Keep It Light   You can also apply light shading by selecting Format Border Shade.

Excel 4 offers two tools that you can use to shade cells. Choose from the Drop Shadow tool on the Drawing Toolbar or Light Shading tool on the Format Toolbar.

Other Formatting Tricks

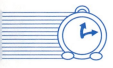

Transfer Formatting   You can quickly transfer formatting from one cell to another by selecting the Paste Formats tool on the Utility Toolbar.

A table, such as the Quarterly Sales Report shown in Figure 16.3, can be quickly formatted by using the AutoFormat tool on the Standard Toolbar. Excel recognizes the standard elements of a table, such as row and column headers, totals, and subtotals. When you use the AutoFormat tool, Excel adds lines, shading and number formatting (based on your preferences) to complete the table. You can change your table formatting preferences with the Format Autoformat command.

In this lesson, you learned some additional tricks to enhance the appearance of your worksheets. In the next lesson, you will learn how to change the sizes of rows and columns.

Lesson 17

Changing Column Width and Row Height

In this lesson, you will learn how to adjust the column width and row height to make best use of the worksheet space. You can set these manually or let Excel make the adjustments for you.

Adjusting Width and Height with the Mouse

To use the mouse to change row height or column width:

1. Move the pointer to the heading for the row or column.

2. Move to the border, as shown in Figure 17.1

3. Drag the border to its new location.

4. Release the mouse button, and the border is reset.

105

Column width change pointer

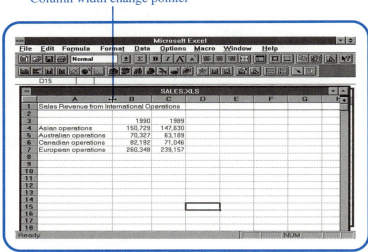

Figure 17.1 Your pointer changes when you move to the border of a row or column.

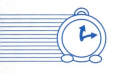 **Custom-Fit Columns** To reset the width for the best fit, double-click on the top right edge of the column. To change more than one column at a time, select as many columns as you like and then place the pointer on the top right edge of the selected columns and double-click.

Using the Keyboard

To use the keyboard to change the column width:

1. Pull down the Format menu.

2. Select Column Width, and the dialog box shown in Figure 17.2 appears.

Figure 17.2   Changing the column width.

3. Type the number of characters you would like as the width. The standard width shown is based on the current default Font.

4. To use the Best Fit, click on the Best Fit button.

5. Click on OK or press Enter.

To use the keyboard to change the row height:

1. Pull down the Format menu.

2. Select Row Height, and the dialog box shown in Figure 17.3 appears.

Figure 17.3   Changing the row height.

3. Type the number of characters you would like as the height. The standard height shown is based on the current default Font.

4. Click on OK or press Enter.

 **Set a New Standard**   To reset the standard width or height, type a new value in the dialog box.

In this lesson, you learned how to change the row height and column width. In the next lesson, you will learn how to use styles.

Lesson 18

Formatting with Styles

In this lesson, you will learn how to use styles when formatting a worksheet.

What Is a Style?

The formats that you have learned to apply individually can be combined into a single step.

Show Your Style   A *style* is a combination of certain formatting attributes.

When you apply a style to a cell or range, any existing attributes will be replaced. Each style can contain the following attributes:

- Number Format

- Font

- Alignment

- Border

- Pattern

- Protection

109

By now, you are familiar with all of these attributes but protection. Protection locks the contents of a cell or range to prevent a change (if the worksheet is also protected) or to hide the cell or range.

Excel has six default styles:

Normal   The default style. Number is set to 0, Font to MS Sans Serif, Size to 10 point, Alignment of numbers is right, and Alignment of text is left, No Border, No Pattern, and Protection is set to locked.

Comma   Number is set to #,##0.00.

Comma (0)   Number is set to #,##0.

Currency   Number is set to $#,##0.00_); (Red) ($#,##0.00).

Currency (0)   Number is set to $#,##0); (Red) ($#,##0).

Percent   Number is set to 0%.

Applying Existing Styles

To apply an existing style to a cell or range using a mouse:

1. Select the cell or range.

2. Click on the down arrow to the right of the Style list box in the Standard Toolbar (see Figure 18.1).

3. Select the style you want from the list. The style is applied to the selected cell or range.

Style list box

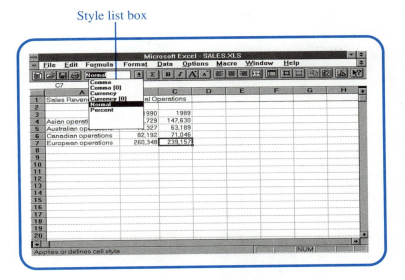

Figure 18.1   The Style list box.

To apply an existing style to a cell or range using the keyboard:

1. Select the cell or range.

2. Pull down the Format menu.

3. Use the arrow keys to select the style you want from the list. The style is applied to the selected cell or range.

Creating Styles

To save time, save your favorite formatting combinations as styles. You can create your own styles by definition, by example, or by copying.

111

To create a style by definition:

1. Pull down the Format menu.

2. Choose Style.

3. Type a name for the style in the **S**tyle Name list box.

4. Click on the Define button, and the dialog box shown in Figure 18.2 appears.

Figure 18.2   Defining a new style.

5. Remove the x from any check box whose attribute you do not want to include in the style.

6. If you want to change the definition of any attribute, click on the appropriate button. For example, to change the Number attribute in the style to $0.00, click on the Number button and change the format.

7. Click on OK or press Enter.

Change 'Em All   If you change the attribute of a style, all cells in that style will also change.

112

To create a new style by example:

1. Select a cell whose format you want to save.

2. Click on the Style list box on the Standard Toolbar.

3. Type a name for the style

4. Press Enter.

To copy existing styles from another worksheet:

1. Open both worksheets.

2. Switch to the worksheet you want to copy the styles to.

3. Pull down the Format menu.

4. Choose Style.

5. Click on the Define button.

6. Click on the Merge button.

7. Select the name of the worksheet to copy from.

8. Click on OK or press Enter to close the Merge dialog box.

9. Click on OK or press Enter.

In this lesson, you learned how to create and apply styles. In the next lesson, you will learn how to create charts.

Lesson 19
Creating Charts

In this lesson, you will learn to create charts to represent your worksheet data graphically.

Charting with Excel

Excel offers you a variety of both two-dimensional and three-dimensional chart types to choose from. A chart can be created as part of your worksheet or as a separate file.

Embedded Charts A chart that is created as part of a worksheet is an embedded chart.

There are two ways to create an embedded chart:

- Use the ChartWizard tool, located on the Standard and Chart Toolbar.

- Use the tools found on the Chart Toolbar.

To create a chart as a separate document that appears in its own window, choose the **New** command on the **File** menu. Select the **Chart** option.

There are several terms that you will encounter when creating a chart:

Data Series A collection of related data, such as the monthly sales for a single division. A data series is usually a single row or column on the worksheet.

Axis One side of a chart. In a two-dimensional chart, there is an x-axis (horizontal) and a y-axis (vertical). In a three-dimensional chart, the z-axis represents the vertical plane, and the x-axis (distance) and y-axis (width) represent the two sides on the floor of the chart.

Legend Defines the separate elements of a chart. For example, the legend for a pie chart will show what each piece of the pie represents.

Choosing the Best Chart Type

Before you learn how to create a chart, take a moment to learn about the different types of charts and how to choose the best chart type for the data you want to graph. A sample of different charts is shown in Figure 19.1.

These are the major chart types and their purposes:

Pie Use this chart to show the relationship between parts of a whole.

Bar Use this chart to compare values at a given point in time.

Column Similar to the Bar chart; use this chart to emphasize the difference between items.

Line Use this chart to emphasize trends and the change of values over time.

Area Similar to the Line chart; use this chart to emphasize the amount of change in values.

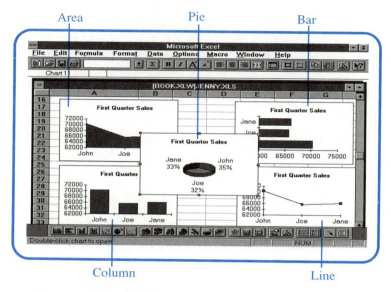

Figure 19.1 Different chart types.

Using the ChartWizard

ChartWizard leads you through the process of creating an embedded chart step-by-step. At each step, you can move back to previous steps and change your choices. ChartWizard will readjust the sample based on your current choices.

To create a chart using the ChartWizard:

1. Select the data you want to chart. Include row and column headings if you want to use them in the chart.

2. Click on the ChartWizard tool on the Standard or Chart Toolbar.

3. Point to the area on the worksheet where you would like to place the chart.

4. Click the left mouse button and hold to drag open the chart area. If you want a square area, hold down the **Shift** key as you drag. If you want your chart to exactly fit the borders of the cells it occupies, hold down the Alt key as you drag. When you have defined the chart area you want, release the mouse button.

5. A dialog box appears, asking you to make changes to the data area of the chart. When it is correct, click on Next or press Enter.

6. Select a chart type from the dialog box, shown in Figure 19.2.

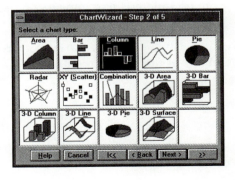

Figure 19.2 ChartWizard asks you to choose the chart type you want.

7. ChartWizard will present you with additional selections, based on the chart type you choose. Complete those selections.

8. ChartWizard will display a sample chart, as shown in Figure 19.3. You may choose whether the data series is based on rows or columns, and choose the starting row and column. Click on Next or press Enter.

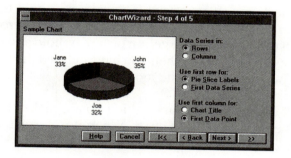

Figure 19.3   ChartWizard prepares a sample chart.

9. Add a legend, title, or axis labels. Click on OK or press Enter. Your completed chart appears on the worksheet.

The Big Move   To move an embedded chart, click anywhere in the chart area and drag it to the new location.

A Bit Cramped   If you did not allow enough room for your chart, simply drag its borders to a new size.

Using the Chart Toolbar

After placing your finished chart on the worksheet, Excel opens the Chart Toolbar. You may use the Chart Toolbar to create a chart, or to change an existing chart. Figure 19.4 shows the Chart Toolbar.

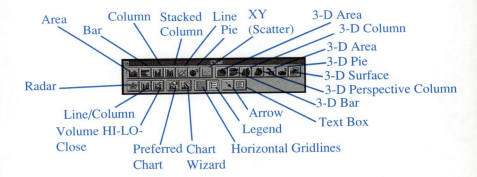

Figure 19.4   The Chart Toolbar.

To use the Chart Toolbar to create a chart:

1. Select the data you want to chart. Include row and column headings if you want to use them in the chart.

2. Click on the tool on the Chart Toolbar which represents the type of chart you want.

3. Point to the area on the worksheet where you would like to place the chart.

4. Click the left mouse button and hold to drag open the chart area. If you want a square area, hold down the Shift key as you drag. If you want your chart to exactly

119

fit the borders of the cells it occupies, hold down the Alt key as you drag. When you have defined the chart area you want, release the mouse button. Excel creates your chart.

Presto!   To quickly change the chart type, click on a different tool on the Chart Toolbar.

Still Not Satisfied?   If you need to make changes to your chart, click on the ChartWizard tool to redefine the data area and make other changes.

Saving Charts

Saving charts is the same as saving a worksheet. If a chart is an embedded chart, it is saved when the worksheet is saved. You can also double-click on an existing chart, and then save that chart in a separate file. If the chart is in a separate document, you must save it separately.

To save a chart in a separate document:

1. Pull down the File menu.

2. Choose Save.

3. If this is a new chart, in the File Name text box, enter the name of the file. You may use any combination of letters or numbers up to eight characters, such as 1992BDGT. Excel will automatically add .XLC to the filename as an extension for a chart. The full filename would then be 1992BDGT.XLC.

4. Click on OK or press Enter.

Printing a Chart

If a chart is an embedded chart, it will print when the worksheet is printed, but you can still print it separately if you want.

To print a chart:

1. If the chart is an embedded chart, open up a chart window by double-clicking on it. If the chart is in a separate file, open that file.

2. Pull down the File menu.

3. Choose Print.

4. Change any print options you would like.

5. Click on OK or press Enter.

Get It Down on Paper   To print a chart quickly, select the Print tool on the Standard Toolbar.

In this lesson, you learned about the different chart types and how to create them. You also learned how to save and print charts. In the next lesson, you will learn how to enhance your charts.

Enhancing Charts

In this lesson, you will learn how to make your charts more appealing.

Resizing a Chart

If you are working on an embedded chart (a chart on a worksheet), prior to adding embellishments, you may want to resize it to allow for more room.

To resize a chart:

1. Select the chart that you want to resize.

2. Click on the border of the chart.

3. Drag the border of the chart to the desired size.

Adding a Title and a Legend

Adding text and a legend to an existing chart is easy.

To add a legend:

1. Select the chart you want to add a legend to.

2. Click on the Legend tool on the Chart Toolbar

3. If necessary, drag the borders of the legend box so that no information is hidden.

You can also add a legend by using the Chart menu, available through the Chart Window. To access the Chart Window, double-click on an embedded chart. Pull down the Chart menu and click on the Add Legends command.

To add a title or other text to a chart:

1. If the chart is an embedded chart, double-click on it to open the Chart Window.

2. Pull down the Chart menu.

3. Choose Attach Text. You can add a chart title, or a title for the x-axis (category), y-axis (series), or z-axis (values). You can also display the value for a data point. A data point is a part of a chart, such as a single column, bar, or plot point for a line. The Attach Text dialog box is shown in Figure 20.1.

Figure 20.1 You can attach text to your chart in many ways.

4. Select the type of text you want to attach and click on OK.

5. Type your text in the formula bar.

If you want to change the font or the alignment or add a border, you must use the Format menu or the Shortcut menu.

You can also add text to the chart or to one of the axes by using the Text tool on the Chart Toolbar. A text box appears on the chart; type text into it. Move the text box and resize it to fit your needs.

 **Point It Out**   You can add arrows to a chart by selecting the Arrow tool on the Chart Toolbar or the Add Arrow option on the Chart menu.

Formatting Text on a Chart

To format text on a chart:

1. Select the text you want to format.

2. Click on the formatting tools on the Standard Toolbar (such as the Bold or Italics tools), or the Formatting Toolbar (such as Font Name or Size). The text changes based on the selections you make. Optionally, you can format text with the Format Text command.

3. If necessary, drag the borders of the text box so that its information shows.

Enhancing the Chart Frame

You can change the border and shading of the chart by using the Forma**t P**atterns command.

To change the border or shading of a chart:

1. Select the chart you want to change.

2. Pull down the Format menu.

3. Choose Patterns.

4. Select the border pattern and shading you want.

5. Click on OK or press Enter.

In this lesson, you learned how to improve the appearance of your chart. In the next lesson, you will learn about 3-D charts.

Lesson 21

Working on 3-D Charts

In this lesson, you will learn how to choose an appropriate 3-D chart.

Choosing a 3-D Chart Type

There are 3-D versions for each of the major chart types: Pie, Bar, Column, Perspective Column, Line, Area, and Surface. Some of these 3-D charts are shown in Figure 21.1.

Use the following as a guide for choosing your 3-D chart:

3-D Pie   Use this type to show the relationship between parts of a whole.

3-D Bar   Use this type to compare values at a given point in time.

3-D Column   Similar to 3-D Bar; use this type to emphasize the difference between items, while allowing easy viewing of data within a series.

3-D Line   Use this type to emphasize trends and the change of values over time. 3-D lines are easier to identify.

3-D Area Similar to 3-D Line; use this type to emphasize the difference between different data series.

3-D Surface Similar to 3-D column; use this to determine the relationships between large amounts of data.

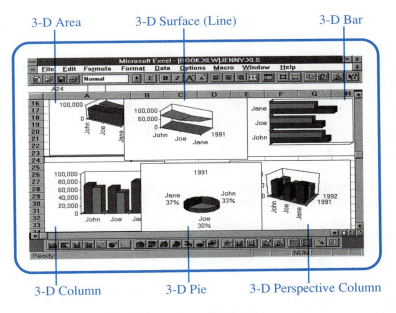

3-D Area   3-D Surface (Line)   3-D Bar

3-D Column   3-D Pie   3-D Perspective Column

Figure 21.1 Examples of 3-D charts.

Creating a 3-D Chart

To create a 3-D chart, follow the same steps as you would in creating a 2-D chart.

To create a 3-D chart using the ChartWizard:

127

1. Select the data you want to chart. Include row and column headings if you want to use them in the chart.

2. Click on the ChartWizard tool on the Standard or Chart Toolbars.

3. Point to the area on the worksheet where you would like to place the chart.

4. Click the left mouse button and hold to drag open the chart area. If you want a square area, hold down the Shift key as you drag. If you want your chart to exactly fit the borders of the cells it occupies, hold down the Alt key as you drag. When you have defined the chart area you want, release the mouse button.

5. A dialog box appears, asking you to make changes to the data area of the chart. When it is correct, click on Next or press Enter.

6. Select a 3-D chart type.

7. ChartWizard will present you with additional selections, based on the chart type you choose. Complete those selections.

8. ChartWizard will display a sample chart. You may choose whether the data series is based on rows or columns, and then choose starting row and column. Click on Next or press Enter.

9. Add a legend, title, or axes titles. Click on OK or press Enter. Your finished chart appears on the worksheet.

You can also use the Chart Toolbar to create a 3-D chart.

Changing the 3-D Chart Type

You can easily change from one 3-D view to another by using the Chart Toolbar.

To change from one 3-D view to another:

1. Select the chart you want to change.

2. Using the Chart Toolbar, click on the 3-D chart tool you want to change to. Excel will change the chart type.

You can also browse through several variations of each chart type in the Chart Gallery.

To access the Chart Gallery:

1. Move to the chart window. If the chart is an embedded chart, then double-click on it to open the chart window.

2. Pull down the Gallery menu.

3. Choose any type of chart from the menu. The Chart Gallery dialog box shown in Figure 21.2 appears.

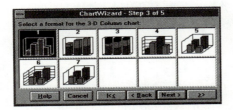

Figure 21.2   Browse among various chart types by using the Chart Gallery dialog box.

Using Multicategory 3-D Charts

When your worksheet has many interrelated values, using a 3-D chart will help you sort the data visually. Suppose you had a worksheet which showed the sales figures for each quarter, for each salesperson. Using a 3-D chart will help you pick out the top sales person for each quarter easily. Such a chart is shown in Figure 21.3.

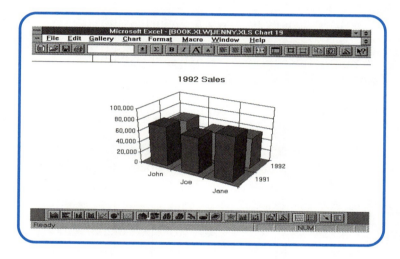

Figure 21.3   A 3-D chart helps you sort out relationships in a complex set of data.

Changing the 3-D Perspective

You might want to change the angle, elevation, or perspective of a 3-D chart in order to make it more pleasing.

To change the 3-D perspective:

1. Select the 3-D chart you want to change. If it is an embedded chart, double-click on it to open the chart window.

2. Pull down the Format menu.

3. Choose 3-D View. The dialog box shown in Figure 21.4 appears.

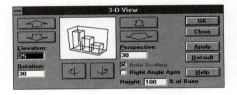

Figure 21.4   Changing the 3-D view.

4. To change the elevation (height from which the chart is seen), click on the up or down elevation controls, or type a number in the Elevation box.

5. To change the rotation (rotation around the z-axis), click on the left or right rotation controls, or type a number in the Rotation box.

6. To change the perspective (perceived depth), click on the up or down perspective controls, or type a number in the Perspective box.

7. As you make changes, they are reflected in the wireframe picture in the middle of the 3-D View dialog box. To see the proposed changes applied to the actual chart, click on the Apply button.

131

8. When you are done making changes, click on OK or press Enter.

In this lesson, you learned how to create a 3-D chart and how to change it to meet your needs. In the next lesson, you will learn how to create a database.

Lesson 22
Creating a Database

In this lesson, you will learn how to create your own database.

Planning a Database

A database is a collection of interrelated records—for example, a checkbook or an address book. Figure 22.1 shows a sample database.

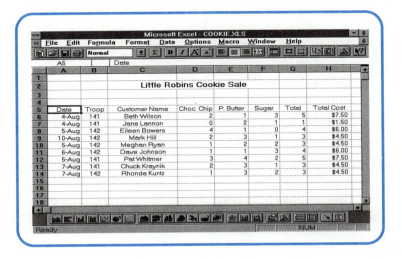

Figure 22.1   Sample database.

Here are some database terms you should be familiar with:

Database Range   The collection of cells that make up the database, including the row and column titles.

Record   The collection of cells (fields) that make up a single item (row) in the database.

Field   Part of a record with a specific type of information. A single column in the row.

Field Name   The name of a field (column heading).

Before you create a database, you should ask yourself a few questions:

- What fields make up an individual record? (Enter the records in rows.) Familiar examples of field information for a database with records about people are name, address, phone number, social security number, and so on.

- What is the most often referenced field in the database? (This field should be placed in the first column.)

- What should the column headings be? (The database works best with column headings that are on a single row.)

- What is the longest value in each column, if you know it? (Use this information to set the column widths. Otherwise you can make your entries and then use Best Fit in the Column Width dialog box to adjust the columns.)

Now you are ready to create a database.

Defining a Database

To create a database:

1. After deciding on the general order of the fields in the database, enter the field (column) headings.

2. Type the individual records (in rows).

3. Select the database area, including the column headings.

4. Pull down the Data menu.

5. Choose Set Database. Excel automatically names the range Database.

Forget Someone?   To add records to a defined database, either add the rows above the last row in the database, or use the Data Form dialog box.

Using Data Forms to Add, Edit, or Delete Records

Data forms are like index cards; there is one data form for each record in the database. It's easier to flip through these data form "cards" than to move among the actual records in your database, so you should use data forms to add, edit, or delete database records.

To access the Data Form dialog box:

1. Pull down the Data menu.

2. Choose Form, and the dialog box shown in Figure 22.2 appears.

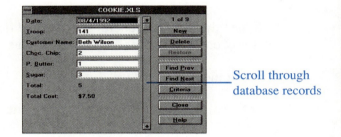

Figure 22.2 The Data Form dialog box.

To add a record to the database:

1. Select the New button.

2. Type data in each of the fields.

3. Click on OK or press Enter.

To change data in a record:

1. Select the record you want to change by selecting the Find Prev or Find Next buttons, or by using the scroll bars to move through the database.

2. Change the data you want, and click on OK or press Enter.

Come Back! To restore data changed in a field before you press Enter, select the Restore button.

To delete a record:

1. Select the record you want to change by selecting the Find Prev or Find Next buttons, or by using the scroll bars to move through the database.

2. Select Delete.

3. Click on OK or press Enter.

In this lesson, you learned how to create a database. In the next lesson, you will learn how to sort the database and find individual records.

Finding and Sorting Data in a Database

In this lesson, you will learn how to sort a database and how to find individual records.

Finding Data with a Data Form

To find records in a database, you must specify the individual criteria (qualifiers). You could type something specific like **Red** under the Color field of the form, or something that must be evaluated, like **<1000** (less than 1000) in the Sales field. Table 23.1 shows the operators that you can use for comparison:

Table 23.1   Excel's Comparison Operators

Operator	Meaning
=	Equal to
>	Greater than
<	Less than
>=	Greater than or equal to
<=	Less than or equal to
<>	Not equal to

You can also use the following wildcards when specifing criteria:

? Represents a single character

* Represents multiple characters

For example, in the Name field, type M* to find everyone whose name begins with an *M*. To find everyone whose three-digit department code has *10* as the last two digits, type ?10.

To find individual records in a database:

1. Pull down the Data menu.

2. Choose Form.

3. Select the Criteria button; the dialog box shown in Figure 23.1 appears.

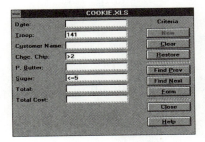

Figure 23.1   Selecting search criteria.

4. Type the criteria you would like to use in the appropriate fields. Use only the fields you want to search.

5. Click on Form or press Enter.

6. Select Find Next or Find Prev to locate certain matching records.

7. When you are done reviewing records, select Close.

Sorting Data in a Database

To sort a database, first decide which field to sort on. For example, an address database could be sorted by Name or by City—or it could be sorted by Name within City within State. Each of these sort fields is considered a *key*.

You can use up to three keys when sorting your database. The first key in the above example would be Name, then City, and then State. You can sort your database in ascending or descending order.

Sort Orders Ascending order is alphabetical (A–Z), and descending order is reverse (Z–A).

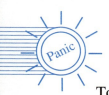

For the Record When you select the database range to sort, include all of the records but not the column headings.

To sort your database:

1. Select the area to be sorted. Make sure to include all of the data in the database but do not include the column headings.

2. Pull down the Data menu.

3. Choose Sort, and the dialog box shown in Figure 23.2 appears.

Figure 23.2   Selecting the sort criteria.

4. Make sure you are sorting by rows, since your database contains its records in rows.

5. Type at least one sort key, and select Ascending or Descending order.

6. Click on OK or press Enter.

Save First   Before sorting, save your database file. Then if the sort does not work out, you still have your original file. If you make a mistake, you can undo the sort by selecting the Undo Sort command on the Edit menu (or press Ctrl-Z).

To sort quickly, use the Sort Ascending or Sort Descending Tools on the Utility Toolbar.

   In this lesson, you learned how to sort your database and how to find individual records. In the next lesson, you will learn how to summarize your database.

Summarizing and Comparing Data in a Database

In this lesson, you will learn how to summarize data in complex databases.

Using the Crosstab ReportWizard

Excel 4 has the ability to create crosstab reports with the Crosstab ReportWizard. It can be used to assemble data from complex databases for analysis. Suppose you had a database which kept track of your sales each day, by product, salesperson, and store. You can create a report which summarized the amount of each product sold at each store by each salesperson.

When you create a crosstab report, you must specify three elements:

Row Fields that form the rows for the report. You can have up to eight rows. For example, these could be *stores*.

Column   Fields that form the column headings for the report. You can have up to eight columns. For example, this could be *salespeople*.

Value   These are the values you want added for each intersection of a column or row. For example, in a crosstab report displaying stores in rows and sales-people in columns, the value added at each intersection could be the amount of CD or record sales (or both) by each salesperson at each store. If you want the number of records that match row and column categories, leave this blank. In our example, this could be *products* or left blank.

A sample database is shown in Figure 24.1.

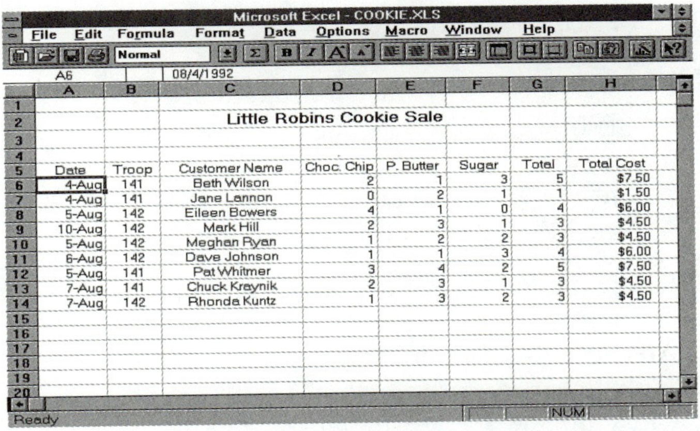

Figure 24.1   A sample database.

Creating a Crosstab Table

To create a crosstab table:

1. Pull down the Data menu.

2. Choose Crosstab.

3. Select the Create a New Crosstab button, and the dialog box shown in Figure 24.2 appears.

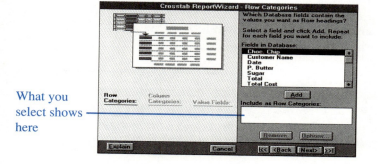

What you
select shows
here

Figure 24.2   Creating a crosstab table.

4. Select the Row, Column, and Value categories.

5. Answer any additional requests for information.

6. Click on the Create It button. Figure 24.3 shows a sample crosstab table.

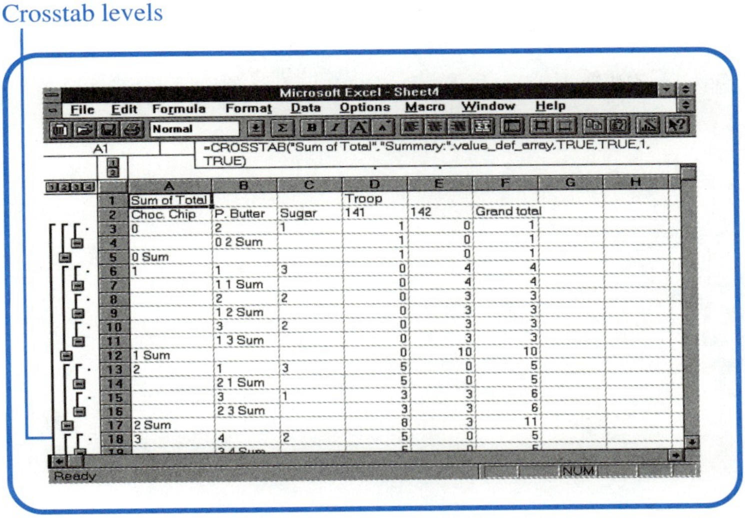

Crosstab levels

Figure 24.3   A sample crosstab table.

Recalculating a Crosstab Table

If you add or change data in a database, you will want to recalculate your crosstab table.

To recalculate a crosstab table:

1. Pull down the Data menu.

2. Choose Crosstab.

3. Choose the Recalculate An Existing Table button.

In this lesson, you learned how to create crosstab reports. In the next lesson, you will learn how to create drawings on your worksheet.

Overtime

Table of Excel Worksheet Functions

Below is a list of the most common Excel built-in functions. The type of data and the order in which it should be typed is included inside the parentheses next to each function. The function syntax is followed by a brief description.

Mathematical Functions

ABS(value)	Calculates the absolue value of a number.
INT(value)	Rounds a number down to the nearest integer.
MOD(dividend, divisor)	Calculates the modulus (remainder) of a divisor and a dividend.
PI()	Used in place of the value pi.
PRODUCT (value, value...)	Calculates the product of the specified values.
ROUND (value, precision)	Rounds a value to a specified number of places.

Statistical Functions

AVERAGE(range) — Calculates the mean average of a group of numbers.

COUNT(range) — Counts the number of cells containing numeric values in a range.

COUNTA(range) — Counts the number of nonblank cells in a range.

MIN(range) — Returns the minimum value in a range of cells.

MAX(range) — Returns the maximum value in a range of cells.

SUM(range) — Calculates the total of a group of cells.

Financial Functions

DDB(cost, salvage, life, period, factor) — Calculates depreciation using the double declining balance method.

FV(interest rate, periods, payment amount, present value, type) — Calculates the future value of an investment.

IPMT(rate, period, periods, present value, future value, type) — Calculates the interest paid for a particular payment.

147

NPER(rate, payment, present value, future value, type)

Calculates the number of payments required to pay off a loan at a given interest rate.

NPV(rate, range)

Calculates the present value of a series of cash flow transactions.

PMT(rate, periods, present value, future value, type)

Calculates the payment amount required for an investment to be paid off given a specific term and interest rate.

PPMT(rate, period, periods, present value, future value, type)

Calculates the amount of principal being paid during any payment period.

RATE(periods, payment, present value, future value, type, guess)

Calculates the interest rate required for a present value to become a greater value.

SLN(cost, salvage, life)

Calculates depreciation using the straight line method.

SYD(cost, salvage, life, period)

Calculates depreciation using the sum of the years' digits method.

Logical Functions

If(condition, value if true, value if false)	Tests whether a condition is true or false.
ISBLANK(cell)	Tests whether a cell is blank.
ISERR(cell)	Tests whether a cell contains an error.

Date and Time Functions

DATEVALUE(text)	Converts a date into a number for use in calculations.
DAY(date)	Returns the day within the date specified.
MONTH(date)	Returns the month within the date specified.
NOW()	Returns the current date and time.
TIMEVALUE(text)	Converts a time into a number for use in calculations.
WEEKDAY(date)	Returns the day of the week based on the date specified.
YEAR(date)	Returns the year within the date specified.

Appendix B

Using DISKCOPY to Make Backups of Program Disks

Before you install any program on your hard disk or run it from your floppy drive, make *backup copies* of the original program disks to avoid damaging the original disks. (Although you don't have to format the blank disks before you begin, the disks must match the program disks in number, size, and density.)

Protect the Disks Before using DISKCOPY, write-protect the original disks. For 3.5" disks, slide the write-protect tab so you can see through the window. For 5.25" disks, apply a write-protect sticker over the write-protect notch.

1. Change to the drive and directory that contains the DOS DISKCOPY file. For example, if the file is in the directory C:\DOS, type `cd\dos` at the C:> prompt and press Enter.

2. Type `diskcopy a: a:` or `diskcopy b: b:`, depending on which drive you're using to make the copies, and press Enter.

3. Insert the original program disk you want to copy into the specified drive and press Enter.

4. Follow the on-screen messages to complete the process.

5. Remove the disk from the drive and label it to match the name of the original program disk.

6. Repeat the process until you have copies of all the program disks.

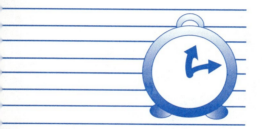

Windows File Manager Primer

Microsoft Windows is a *graphical user interface* (GUI) which runs on top of DOS (your computer's Disk Operating System). Although many users consider the Windows screen (interface) easier to use, you need to know how to use it before it will seem easy.

Graphical User Interface? With a graphical user interface, you don't type commands. Instead, you use a pointing device, usually a mouse, to select the command from a menu or to select a graphic symbol (icon) from the screen.

In addition to a graphical interface, Windows offers a *multitasking* environment. This means that you can run two or more programs at the same time (each in a separate window) and smoothly switch from one program to the other.

Starting Windows

To start Windows, follow these steps:

1. Change to the drive that contains your Windows files. For example, type **c:** at the DOS prompt and press Enter.

2. Change to the directory that contains your Windows files. For example, if the name of the directory is WINDOWS, type `cd\windows` at the prompt and press Enter.

3. Type `win` and press Enter. DOS starts Windows. The Windows title screen appears for a few moments, and then you see the Program Manager screen.

Managing Directories and Files with the Windows File Manager

Windows includes a special program called the File Manager, which simplifies many of the DOS file-related tasks, including listing, copying, and deleting files. To open the File Manager, double-click on the File Manager icon in the Main Program Group window. Or, use the arrow keys to highlight the File Manager icon, then press Enter to start it. If the Main window is not shown, pull down the Window menu and select Main. The following list tells you how to move around in the File Manager.

- To change drives, click on the drive letter at the top of the Directory Tree window. Or, press the Tab key to move up to the drive list, highlight a drive letter with the arrow keys, and press Enter.

- To display the subdirectories of a directory, click on the plus sign to the left of the directory's name, or highlight the directory and press the + (plus) key. To reverse the process, press the - (hyphen) key or click on the minus sign.

- To open a directory, double-click on it or high' and press Enter. You can open more than one di window at a time.

- To activate a directory window, click anywhere on the window or use Ctrl-Tab to switch windows.

- To close the File Manager, pull down the File menu and select Exit, or double-click on the Control Menu box in the upper left corner of the screen.

Making Directories with the File Manager

1. Highlight the directory under which you want the new directory.

2. Pull down the File menu and select Create Directory.

3. Type the name of the new directory in the dialog box.

4. Click on OK or press Enter.

Selecting Files To Copy, Move, or Delete

Before you can copy, move, or delete files, you must select the files using one of the following methods.

With the Mouse:

- To select a group of consecutive files, hold down the Shift key and click on the first and last files in the group.

- To select a group of nonconsecutive files, hold down the Ctrl key and click on each file. To deselect a file, click on it again.

With the Keyboard:

- To select a group of consecutive files, highlight the first file, hold down the Shift key, and use the arrow keys to stretch the highlight over the desired group.

- To select a group of nonconsecutive files, press Shift-F8, and then select each file by highlighting it and pressing the space bar. To deselect a file, highlight it and press the space bar.

Copying Files

1. Select the files you want to copy.

2. Pull down the File menu and select Copy, or press F8. The Copy dialog box appears.

3. Type the destination drive, directory, and file name in the To: text box.

4. Press the Copy button. Windows copies the file to the location you specified.

Moving Files

1. Activate the directory window for the directory that contains the files you want to move.

2. Select the files you want to move.

3. Pull down the File menu and select Move, or press F7. The Move dialog box appears, prompting you to specify a destination directory for the selected files.

4. Type a complete path to the destination directory, and then press the Move button. The selected files are moved to the destination directory you specified.

Deleting Files

1. Select the files you want to delete.

2. Pull down the File menu and select Delete. The Delete dialog box appears prompting you to confirm the operation.

3. Press the Delete button to delete the selected files or Cancel to cancel the operation.

For More Information...

For more information about using Windows 3.1, try these other books from Sams:

The *10 Minute Guide to Windows 3.1,* by Kate Barnes.

The First Book of Windows 3.1, Second Edition, by Jack Nimersheim.

Index